ELEVENTH EDITION

CLASSROOM READING INVENTORY

WARREN H. WHEELOCK

University of Missouri–Kansas City

NICHOLAS J. SILVAROLI

Late of Arizona State University

CONNIE J. CAMPBELL

Campbell-Wheelock Interventions

 **McGraw-Hill**
Higher Education

Boston   Burr Ridge, IL   Dubuque, IA   New York   San Francisco   St. Louis
Bangkok   Bogotá   Caracas   Kuala Lumpur   Lisbon   London   Madrid   Mexico City
Milan   Montreal   New Delhi   Santiago   Seoul   Singapore   Sydney   Taipei   Toronto

McGraw-Hill Higher Education

McGraw-Hill Higher Education
 A Division of The McGraw-Hill Companies

Published by McGraw-Hill, an imprint of The McGraw-Hill Companies, Inc., 1221 Avenue of the Americas, New York, NY 10020. Copyright © 2009, 2004, 1997, 1986, 1982. All rights reserved. No part of this publication may be reproduced or distributed in any form or by any means, or stored in a database or retrieval system, without the prior written consent of The McGraw-Hill Companies, Inc., including, but not limited to, in any network or other electronic storage or transmission, or broadcast for distance learning.

This book is printed on acid-free paper.

1 2 3 4 5 6 7 8 9 0 QPD/QPD 0 9 8

ISBN: 978-0-07-313127-6
MHID: 0-07-313127-X

Editor in Chief: *Michael Ryan*
Publisher: *Beth Mejia*
Sponsoring Editor: *Allison McNamara*
Marketing Manager: *Rebecca Saidlower*
Developmental Editor: *Marley Magaziner*
Project Manager: *Amanda Peabody*
Manuscript Editors: *Patterson Lamb / Sharon O'Donnell*
Design Manager: *Andrei Pasternak*
Cover Designer: *Asylum Studios*
Production Supervisor: *Louis Swaim*
Composition: *Laserwords Private Limited*
Printing: *45# Pub New Era Matte Plus Recycled, Quebecor World Dubuque*

Cover: © David Buffington / Photodisc / Getty Images

Library of Congress Cataloging-in-Publication Data

Wheelock, Warren.
  Classroom Reading Inventory / Warren Wheelock, Connie Campbell, Nicholas Silvaroli.—11th ed.
    p. cm.
  ISBN-13: 978-0-07-313127-6 (alk. paper)
  ISBN-10: 0-07-313127-X (alk. paper)
  1. Reading—Ability testing. 2. Reading (Elementary) I. Campbell, Connie. II. Silvaroli, Nicholas. III. Title.
LB1050.46.S53 2008
372.48—dc22

                                                         2007047178

The Internet addresses listed in the text were accurate at the time of publication. The inclusion of a Web site does not indicate an endorsement by the authors or McGraw-Hill, and McGraw-Hill does not guarantee the accuracy of the information presented at these sites.

w.mhhe.com

DEDICATION

Nicholas J. Silvaroli
1930–1995

*I count myself in nothing else so happy as in a
soul remembering my good friend.*

Wm. Shakespeare—King Richard II

CONTENTS

PREFACE

The Classroom Reading Inventory (CRI) is specially prepared for inservice teachers and preservice teachers who have little or no experience with informal reading inventories.

The CRI is a leading reading diagnostic tool because of its ease of use and time-saving administration. If you follow these recommendations, you will gain the information and confidence for mastery of the CRI:

- Read the entire manual carefully.
- Study the specific instructions thoroughly.
- Get started with the basics by administering the CRI to at least three students.

Your skill and success with individual diagnostic reading techniques are developed gradually through experience. You will find that the techniques, procedures, and ideas must be adapted to each student and testing situation, for no two are alike.

After administering the CRI seven to ten times, you will find yourself more and more adept in understanding, documenting, and interpreting the reader's responses. Most important, you will see your teaching improve because you will align your instruction more clearly and precisely with the reading needs, levels, skills, and comprehension priorities of your students.

As with previous editions of the CRI, you will see that Form A follows a subskills format, and Form B follows a reader response format. Both forms include pretests and posttests.

What's New in This Edition?

We have made the following changes, additions, and modifications to this edition based on feedback from CRI users:

- **Multicultural stories and themes:** More than 20 percent of the stories are new and updated, with expanded emphasis on multicultural characters and global themes.
- **Online high school and adult testing material:** The diagnostic and subskills material for high school and adult education students is now available online at www.classroomreadinginventory .com.
- **Online video clips and explanations:** Video clips of the CRI being administered and explanations and other resources for future teachers also are now available on the Web site www .classroomreadinginventory.com.
- **Favorite features streamlined and improved:** Also included are improved formatting of word lists, correction of ambiguous items, reduction of the length of some stories, and improvement of selected questions.
- **Web-based support and information from the authors:** The authors are pleased to provide through this edition more personalized assistance and information at www.classroom readinginventory .com, where you can access FAQs, case studies utilizing the CRI, and an e-mail address for communications and questions.

ACKNOWLEDGMENTS

We would like to thank the following reviewers whose comments helped form this revision.

Sally Barnhart, Xavier University

Tim Croy, Eastern Illinois University

Jo Ann Karr, Northeastern Illinois University

Leana B. McClain, Indiana University

Marilyn Mudge, Wayne State College

Priscilla Myers, Santa Clara University

Kristen R. Pennycuff, Tennessee Technological
University

Janice Pilgreen, University of La Verne

Pamela Pretty, Western Kentucky University

Patsy Self, Florida International University

Peggy L. Snowden, SUNY Plattsburgh

Jennifer Stone, University of Washington

Bruce A. Wisowaty, Calumet College of Saint Joseph

INTRODUCTION

What Is an Informal Reading Inventory (IRI)?

An informal reading inventory (IRI) is a set of graded word lists and passages used to estimate students' oral and silent reading skills. Searfoss, Readance, and Mallette (2001) write, "In the hands of a skilled examiner, the IRI is one of the best diagnostic instruments available. The major advantage of the IRI is that it enables the examiner to observe a child in the act of reading. Specifically, it yields information about both word recognition and comprehension that is not readily provided by standardized group tests. In addition to supplying valuable quantitative data, the IRI offers the opportunity to examine qualitative aspects of a child's performance. For example, behaviors such as a slow reading rate and word-by-word reading may be important indicators of difficulty. Also, by analyzing the types of errors the child makes when reading orally, the teacher gets a better insight into the strategies being used to interpret text."[1]

What Is the Classroom Reading Inventory (CRI)?

The CRI is an individual diagnostic reading test providing information to teachers that will enable them to make instructional decisions. It is designed to be used with elementary, junior high/middle school, high school, and adult education students. The CRI employs two main formats: SUBSKILLS FORMAT and READER RESPONSE FORMAT.

SUBSKILLS FORMAT

At the elementary and junior/middle school levels, the Subskills Format enables the teacher to diagnose a student's ability to decode words (word recognition) both in isolation and in context and to answer questions (comprehension). In addition, the Subskills Format provides the teacher with a pretest and a posttest. The Subskills Format logically follows the type of reading instructional program being used in most elementary and junior high/middle schools.

At the high school and adult education levels, the Subskills Format enables the teacher to also diagnose a student's ability to decode words and to answer questions.

READER RESPONSE FORMAT

A number of classroom reading programs have shifted from a subskills instructional emphasis to a literacy emphasis. The Reader Response Format follows the type of literacy program that challenges students to use their inferential and critical reading and thinking abilities. The Reader Response Format

---

[1]   Searfoss, Lyndon W.; Readance, John E.; and Mallette, Marla H. *Helping Children Learn to Read,* 4th ed. Allyn & Bacon, Boston, 2001, p. 124.

provides the teacher with a pretest and a posttest for use with elementary and junior high/middle school students.

HIGH SCHOOL AND ADULT EDUCATION SUBSKILLS MATERIAL

This edition *does not* include diagnostic subskills material for high school and adult education students. However, the diagnostic subskills material for high school and adult education students can be downloaded from the Web site www.classroomreadinginventory.com.

Purpose of the Classroom Reading Inventory

Norm-referenced tests, like the Iowa Test of Basic Skills, are used to determine student reading achievement. This is a group testing approach that can be termed *classification testing*. The results from these group tests classify students according to a global reading achievement level, which is usually interpreted as a student's instructional reading level. The Classroom Reading Inventory (CRI), a version of an informal reading inventory, is an individual testing procedure that enables the teacher to identify a student's reading skills or abilities or both.

Differences Between Individual and Group Testing

The differences between individual and group testing can be illustrated by a brief description of the reading performances of two fifth-grade students, Eleni and Marco. Their norm-referenced test (NRT) results are

> Eleni (10 years 9 months old): NRT 4.2 overall reading
> Marco (11 years 2 months old): NRT 4.2 overall reading

When we examine their NRT results, these two fifth-grade students appear to be about the same in age and overall reading achievement. However, data obtained from their individual CRIs indicate that there are significant *instructional* differences between these two students.

On the Graded Word Lists, Part 1 of the CRI, Eleni correctly pronounced all words at all grade levels, one through eight inclusive. It is evident that Eleni is well able to "sound out" or "decode" words. However, when Eleni read the Graded Paragraphs, Part 2, she was unable to answer many of the questions about these stories even at a first-grade-reader level of difficulty. Eleni is what is known as a *word caller*. That is, Eleni is quite proficient at decoding words but she does not assign meaning to the words she decodes.

Marco, on the other hand, was able to answer questions about these same stories up to a fourth-grade-reader level of difficulty. However, his phonetic and structural analysis, or decoding, skills were inadequate for his level of development. Marco is what is known as a *context reader*. That is, even though his decoding skills are inadequate, he can usually answer questions based on the words he does decode and his background knowledge of the material.

The results obtained from an NRT concerning reading achievement tend to *classify* students as average, above average, or below average in terms of their reading achievement. While the results of an NRT may tell the teacher that a student is below average in reading, they cannot tell why the student is below average. These tests are not diagnostic. Therefore, as teachers, we need much more specific information about a student's decoding and comprehension skills if we are to be able to develop meaningful *independent* and *instructional* reading programs for every student. An informal reading inventory does what an inventory is supposed to do—take stock. If a teacher knows what a student has in the way of phonetic and structural analysis skills, for example, then the teacher also knows what phonetic and structural analysis skills the student doesn't have. The same applies to the area of comprehension. The CRI is designed to provide teachers with just such specific and necessary diagnostic information.

GENERAL INFORMATION

Brief Overview

What follows is a brief overview of the formats and forms used in the eleventh edition of the CRI.

SUBSKILLS FORMAT (elementary, junior high/middle school)
Form A: Pretest
Form A: Posttest

READER RESPONSE FORMAT (elementary, junior high/middle school)
Form B: Pretest
Form B: Posttest

SUBSKILLS FORMAT (high school and adult)
Form C: Pretest
Form C: Posttest
These forms are available for downloading at www.classroomreadinginventory.com.

How Does the Subskills Format Differ from the Reader Response Format?

- SUBSKILLS FORMAT: The Subskills Format enables the teacher to evaluate the student's ability to decode words in and out of context, and to evaluate the student's ability to answer factual/literal, vocabulary, and inference questions.
- READER RESPONSE FORMAT: The Reader Response Format enables the teacher to evaluate various aspects of the student's comprehension ability by means of the following procedure. First, the student is asked to use the story title to *predict* what the story will be about. Second, the student is asked to *retell* the story or text with an emphasis on character(s), problem(s), and outcome(s)/solution(s).
- SUBSKILLS FORMAT: Both formats use a *quantitative* scale for the evaluation of a student's reading ability. In the Subskills Format, if the student answers correctly four of the five questions, the student is considered to be *independent* in comprehension at that level. This format evaluates the student's ability to answer questions correctly.
- READER RESPONSE FORMAT: In the Reader Response Format a number is assigned to the *quality* of the responses given by the student. For example, when the student is discussing character(s), the student is given zero credit for no response and three points if, in the teacher's judgment, the student's response is on target. The Reader Response Format is designed to enable the teacher to evaluate the student's ability to predict and retell narrative or expository texts.

Are There Other Differences?

- SUBSKILLS FORMAT: Using the Subskills Format the teacher records correct and incorrect student responses and evaluates these responses to determine subskills needs in word recognition and comprehension.

- READER RESPONSE FORMAT: The Reader Response Format requires the teacher to direct the student to make predictions about the story and to ask the student to retell what s/he can about the character(s), problem(s), and outcome(s)/solution(s) of the story. The teacher evaluates the student's thinking in terms of how the student makes inferences and summarizes information, to mention just two examples.

Are There Ways in Which These Formats Are Similar?

- Both the Subskills Format and the Reader Response Format provide the teacher with authentic information. Both formats establish instructional reading levels.

Is the CRI Used with Groups or Individuals?

- Within both formats, all six forms are to be used with individual students.

What Is Meant by Background Knowledge Assessment?

- A student's background knowledge plays a crucial part in the reading comprehension process. Gunning (1998) writes, "Preparational strategies are those that a reader uses to prepare for reading. These include activating prior knowledge . . . and setting a goal for reading. [With] failure to activate prior knowledge, poor readers may not connect information in the text with what they already know."[2] It follows that the teacher should make a quick assessment of the student's background (prior) knowledge before the student is asked to read any narrative or expository material. Furthermore, the teacher should consider the amount of background (prior) knowledge when determining the levels.

Why Are Administrative Time and Cost Important Factors in the CRI?

- Teachers generally have only limited time to test individual students. With this in mind, each form of the CRI is designed to be administered in *fifteen minutes or less.* However, more time is needed when learning to administer the CRI. Cost is kept to a minimum by permitting teachers to reproduce the Inventory Record for all six forms.

What Readability Formula Was Used in the Development of the CRI?

- For the Subskills Format Form A: Pretest and Posttest, and the Reader Response Format Form B: Pretest and Posttest, the Harris-Jacobson Wide Range Readability Formula[3] was used. This is also the case for the high school and adult Subskills Format.

How Were the Graded Paragraphs Developed and Accuracy Ensured?

- All of the stories for the Graded Paragraphs are original stories written by the authors. All of the stories have been field tested to ensure accurate level material has been written.

---

[2]   Gunning, Thomas B. *Assessing and Correcting Reading and Writing Difficulties.* Allyn & Bacon, Boston, 1998, p. 314.

[3]   Harris, Albert J., and Sipay, Edward R. *How to Increase Reading Ability,* 8th ed. Longman, New York, 1985, pp. 656–673.

A WORD TO THE WISE

1. When administering the Classroom Reading Inventory, a right-handed teacher seems to have better control of the testing situation by placing the student to the left, thus avoiding the problem of having the inventory record forms between them.

2. When administering Part 2 (Graded Paragraphs), the teacher should remove the student booklet before asking the questions on the comprehension check. Thus, the student is encouraged to utilize recall ability rather than merely locate answers in the material just read.

3. The word count given in parentheses at the top of each paragraph in the Inventory Record for Teachers does not include the words in the title.

4. Students living in different parts of the United States may react differently to the Graded Paragraphs. If you or your students react negatively to one or more of the paragraphs, feel free to interchange the paragraphs contained in the Pre- and Posttests.

5. It is important to establish rapport with the student being tested. Avoid using words such as *test* or *test taking.* Instead use *working with words, saying words for me,* or *talking about stories.*

6. Before the teacher can analyze the types of word recognition errors a student makes, s/he will need a basic understanding of the word recognition concepts listed on the Inventory Record Summary sheet such as blends, digraphs, short vowels. (See p. 168 for a reference regarding basic word recognition concepts.)

7. When a student hesitates or cannot pronounce a word within 5 seconds in Part 2 (Graded Paragraphs), the teacher should *quickly* pronounce that word to maintain the flow of the oral reading.

8. Testing on the Graded Paragraphs of Form A, Part 2, should be discontinued when the student reaches the Frustration Level in *either* word recognition or comprehension.

9. The Inventory Record for all formats can be downloaded from www.classroomreadinginventory.com. Also, your test copies have been laminated so that they will remain in pristine condition.

10. Any of the Graded Paragraphs, Forms A, B, and C from the Subskills Format, can be used as silent reading selections. Tell the student he is to read the story silently and that you will still be asking him the questions. Before starting, do the Background Knowledge Assessment.

11. The scoring guide on Form A, Pretest and Posttest, Part 2, of the Inventory Record for Teachers may cause some interpretation problems. As an example, let's look at the scoring guide for the story "Our Bus Ride" from Form A, Part 2, Primer.

SIG WR Errors		COMP Errors	
IND (Independent)	0	IND (Independent)	0–1
INST (Instructional)	3	INST (Instructional)	1 ½–2
FRUST (Frustration)	6+	FRUST (Frustration)	2 ½+

Should IND or INST be circled if a student makes one or two significant word recognition errors? It is the authors' opinion that (a) if the student's comprehension is at the independent level, select the independent level for word recognition; (b) if in doubt, select the lowest level. This practice is referred to as *undercutting.* If the teacher undercuts or underestimates the student's instructional level, the chances of success at the initial point of instruction increase.

At any rate, it is the teacher who makes the decision. To help you make this decision, take into account those *qualitative* features such as, was it a fluent and expressive reading, or was it word-by-word? When you take into account *qualitative* features there will be less confusion as to which level to indicate. Remember: It is you the teacher who makes the decision—not the test.

USING THE CRI:
SPECIFIC INSTRUCTIONS

For Administering the Subskills Format
Form A: Pretest and Form A: Posttest

PART 1 Graded Word Lists: Subskills Format

Purposes:
1. To identify specific word recognition errors.
2. To estimate the starting level at which the student begins reading the Graded Paragraphs in Part 2.

Procedure: Always begin Part 1 Graded Word Lists at the preprimer (PP) level. Present the Graded Word Lists to the student and say:

> "I have some words on these lists, and I want you to say them out loud for me. If you come to a word you don't know, it's OK to say—'I don't know.' Just do the best you can."

Discontinue at the level at which the student mispronounces or indicates s/he does not know five of the twenty words at a particular grade level (75 percent). Each correct response is worth five points.

As the student pronounces the words at each level, the teacher should record all word responses on the Inventory Record for Teachers.[1] Self-corrected errors are counted as acceptable responses in Part 1. These recorded word responses may be analyzed later to determine specific word recognition needs.

How to Record Student Responses to the Graded Word Lists

1. came   ✓   The checkmark (✓) means the student decoded the word *came* correctly.

2. liberty *library*   The student decoded the word *liberty* as *library*.

3. stood   *P*   The *P* means the student did not respond to the word *stood* and the teacher pronounced it to maintain an even flow.

4. car $\overset{+}{can}$ Initially, the student decoded *car* as *can* but quickly corrected the error. This is a self-corrected error as indicated by the + sign.

5. turkeys Ⓢ   The Ⓢ means the student left off the *s* in *turkeys*, and pronounced it as *turkey*. Anything circled on the CRI indicates where something has been omitted.

6. chase   *d*   The *d* not encircled means the student added a *d* to the word *chase* and pronounced it as *chased*. The use of an encircled omitted ending, or an uncircled added word ending, enables the teacher to speed up the recording process.

7. guides *gēds*   The student decoded the word *guides* by using a nonsense word. When this happens, record a phonetic approximation of the nonsense word given. In this example, the student said *gēds*.

---

[1] The Inventory Record for Teachers is a separate record form printed on standard 8 1/2 × 11 paper. *Note:* Teachers may download from the Inventory Record for Teachers at www.classroomreadinginventory.com.

PART 2 Graded Paragraphs: Subskills Format

Purposes:
1. To estimate the student's independent and instructional levels. Also, to identify the student's frustration level and, if necessary, the student's listening capacity level.
2. To identify significant word recognition errors made during oral reading and to determine the extent to which the student actually comprehends what s/he reads.

Procedure: Present the Graded Paragraphs starting at the highest level at which the student decoded correctly all twenty words on the Graded Word Lists, Part 1, and say:

> "I have some stories here that I want you to read out loud to me. After you finish a story, I will ask you some questions about what you read."

At this point introduce each story to be read by completing the Background Knowledge Assessment (e.g., say "This story is about puppies. What can you tell me about puppies?").

Levels

What follows is a brief explanation of each of the four *levels* that apply to Subskills Format Form A. These four levels are referred to as Independent (IND), Instructional (INST), Frustration (FRUST), and Listening Capacity (LC).

Independent Level

The independent level is defined as adequate functioning in reading with no help from the teacher. Adequate functioning means 99 percent accuracy in word recognition and with 90 percent comprehension or better.[2] The teacher will use the independent level estimate in selecting supplementary reading material and the library and trade books students can read comfortably on their own. Since this is the type of reading students will be doing for personal recreation and information, it is important that the students be given reading material from which they can extract content without the hazards of unfamiliar words and concepts.

Instructional Level

As the selections become more difficult, the student will reach a level at which s/he can read with at least 95 percent accuracy in word recognition and with 75 percent comprehension or better. At this level the student needs the teacher's help. This is the student's instructional level, useful in determining the level of textbook that can be read with some teacher guidance.

Frustration Level

When the student reads a selection that is beyond the recommended instructional level, the teacher may well observe symptoms of frustration such as anxiety, tension, excessive finger-pointing, and slow, halting, word-by-word reading. Word recognition accuracy drops to 90 percent or lower. Comprehension may be extremely poor, with 50 percent or lower accuracy. Usually most of the concepts and questions are inaccurately discussed by the student. This represents a level that should be avoided when textbooks and supplementary reading material are being selected.

---

[2] The actual number of significant word recognition and comprehension errors permissible at each grade level can be found in the separate Inventory Record for Teachers.

Listening Capacity Level

For the novice CRI user, when and how to administer the listening capacity assessment can be confusing.

The listening capacity level is defined as adequate understanding of material that is read to the student by the examiner. This is done to determine whether the student can understand and discuss what s/he listened to at levels beyond the frustration level. It is assumed that the reading skills might be improved through further instruction, at least to the listening capacity level. A score of 70 percent or better is an indication of adequate understanding.

Not all students are administered the listening capacity assessment. For when, and when not, to use the listening capacity assessment see the sample CRI records on p. 31.

When the teacher makes a decision that a student has reached the frustration level in either word recognition and/or comprehension, this part of the testing is concluded. The teacher then decides whether to go to the listening capacity format. To see how one teacher makes this decision check the sample CRI records on p. 39.

GENERAL INTRODUCTION TO MISCUE ANALYSIS

Recording Word Recognition Errors

In 1982, Pikulski and Shanahan[1] reviewed research on informal reading inventories. One of their conclusions was that "errors should be analyzed both qualitatively and quantitatively."

There was a time when it was assumed that all word recognition errors were of equal significance: an error is an error is an error. As such, the teacher was asked merely to *quantify,* or count, all word recognition errors and regard them as equal. The CRI requires the teacher to count errors (quantitative) and also to reflect about what the student actually is doing as s/he makes the error (qualitative); that is, what caused the student to make the error?

In general, a word recognition error should be judged as *significant* (high-weighted) if the error impacts or interferes with the student's fluency or thought process. *Insignificant* (low-weighted) word recognition errors are minor alterations and do not interfere with student fluency or cognition; for example, the student substitutes *a* for *the* before a noun or infrequently omits or adds a word ending. These are very common miscues.

The following examples are designed to enable teachers to make qualitative judgments of significant and insignificant word recognition errors. It is impossible, however, to account for all possibilities. With this in mind, teachers are advised to use this information as a guide to establish their own criteria for developing a qualitative mind-set by which to determine whether a word recognition error is significant or insignificant. The more a teacher thinks about what caused an error, the better that teacher will be able to understand the decoding process.

Significant and Insignificant Word Recognition Errors

The following are examples of common word recognition error types.

- **Example:** The turkey is a silly bird.

  P

The student does not recognize a word and *needs teacher assistance.* This is symbolized by placing a *P* (for *pronounced*) over the word not recognized. This is always regarded as a significant error.

- **Example:** The cat chased the birds. OR It was a very hot day.

The student *omits* a word or part of a word. This is symbolized by drawing a circle around the omitted word or word part. Infrequent omissions are considered insignificant word recognition errors. Frequent omissions, however, are significant. There is no definite number that indicates infrequent/frequent omissions. Only you the teacher, as you listen to the student read, can determine what is infrequent/frequent. The teacher is the decision maker.

---

[1] Pikulski, John, and Shanahan, Timothy. "Informal Reading Inventories: A Critical Analysis" in *Approaches to Informal Evaluation of Reading.* John J. Pikulski and Timothy Shanahan, eds. International Reading Association, Newark, DE.

- **Example:**   *Significant:*   Baby birds like to eat seeds and ~~grain~~. *grin*

                Insignificant: He went to ~~the~~ store. OR *a*

                The children were lost in the ~~forest~~. *woods*

The student *substitutes* a word for the word as given. This is symbolized by writing the word substituted above the word as given. This type of error is judged to be significant if it impacts or interferes with fluency or cognition. However, it may also be judged as insignificant if it does not interfere with fluency or cognition.

- **Example:**   *Significant:*   The trees ^ look small. *don't*

                Insignificant: The trees look ^ small. *so*

The student *inserts* a word into the sentence. This is symbolized by the use of a caret (^) with the inserted word above the caret. Insertions are usually regarded as insignificant word recognition errors because they tend to embellish what the student is reading. However, if the insertion changes the meaning of what is being read, it should be judged as significant.

- **Example:**   *Significant:*   They were bound ⁀for the salt springs⁀ near the mountains.

                Insignificant: The crowd ⁀at the⁀ rodeo stood up.

The student repeats a word or words. This is symbolized by drawing an arc over the repeated word(s). Repetitions are usually considered to be insignificant errors if they are infrequent. However, excessive repetitions suggest the need for more reading practice, and they should be judged as significant. What is infrequent/excessive is the teacher's decision.

As teachers become accustomed to thinking qualitatively about why students make the errors they do, they will become more sensitive to a qualitative analysis of word recognition errors. As such, teachers will begin to better understand the decoding process and what mediates error behavior. The following are examples of enhanced sensitivity on the part of teachers regarding qualitative analysis.

- **Example:** The bird~~s~~ ~~are~~ singing. *is*

This is an example of omission and word substitution. The first error, omitted *s*, caused the second error, substituting *is* for *are*. If the student did not substitute *is* for *are*, language dissonance would occur.

- **Example:** How high ~~we are~~? *are we*

This shows two word substitution errors of a reversal word order. These errors were caused by the first word *How. How,* at the beginning of a sentence, usually signals to the reader that it will be a question. This is just what the reader did: anticipated a question and made it into a question. This counts as only one error.

- **Example:** ~~It is~~ a work car. *It's*

Here two words are contracted because it is more natural to say *it's* than *it is.* Remember, it's not a case of how many errors (quantitative) but, rather, what causes the errors (qualitative). The more you become accustomed to thinking about errors, the better you will be able to understand the decoding process.

As the authors indicated in the introduction to this section, it is impossible to account for all possible miscues. Some miscues are errors of anticipation. For example, a student is reading a sentence and s/he senses that a noun is coming up. The student also knows that before that noun there will be either the definite article *the,* or the indefinite article *a.* Sensing the approach of the noun the student, in this example, anticipates the definite article *the.* Even if it turns out that the article is the indefinite *a,* the student is likely to read *the,* for this is what s/he anticipated. The reverse is also true.

Language or regional dialect differences can also be miscues and should not be regarded as decoding errors, but as language differences. For example, a student comes to the word *fingers* on the Graded Word Lists. S/he read *fingers* as *fangers.* How can we be sure, then, that this is due to language differences and not a decoding error. Easy, the teacher asks, "what are *fangers.*" The student holds up a hand and says, "*these are my fangers.*" Dialect, not decoding!

Students whose first language is Spanish typically have difficulty with the way in English the *ch* and *sh* sounds are articulated. As such, the English as a second language (ESL) student may decode the word *chair* as *share.* Language difficulty, not decoding!

Marking Word Recognition Errors on Graded Paragraphs

- **Example:** Elephants are unusual animals. *(P above "Elephants")*

Student does not recognize a word. Teacher pronounces the word for the student and marks it with a *P.*

- **Example:** We are ~~ready~~ to go now. *(riding above "ready")*

Student substitutes a word for the word as given. Teacher writes the substituted word above the given word.

- **Example:** After week(s) of hunting . . .

- **Example:** It was a (good) day for a ride.

Student omits a word(s) or a word part. Teacher draws a circle around the omitted word(s) or word part.

- **Example:** Mike is John's ^ friend. *(best above the caret)*

Student inserts a word into the body of a sentence. Teacher uses a caret to show where the word was inserted.

- **Example:** It was a good day for a ride. *(arcs over "It was" and "a ride")*

Student repeats a word(s). Teacher draws an arc over the repeated word(s).

Evaluating Comprehension Responses

After each graded paragraph, the student is asked to answer questions. The separate Inventory Record for Teachers labels questions as follows:

(F) Factual or Literal
(I) Inference
(V) Vocabulary

Suggested answers are listed after each question. However, these answers are to be read as guides or probable answers. The teacher must judge the adequacy of each response made by the student. In most cases it is helpful to record student responses if they differ from the listed suggested responses.

Scoring Guide

What follows is the scoring guide used for the story "Pirates!" fifth-grade level, Form A: Pretest.

Scoring Guide	Fifth		
SIG WR Errors		**COMP Errors**	
IND	2	IND	0–1
INST	8	INST	1 ½–2
FRUST	17+	FRUST	2 ½+

The scoring guide for this level, as well as all other levels in Part 2 Graded Paragraphs, uses error limits for the reader—in other words, Independent (IND), Instructional (INST), and Frustration (FRUST) reading levels.

As such, the guide suggests that when a student reads "Pirates!" and makes two Significant (SIG) Word Recognition (WR) errors, the student is able to Independently (IND) decode typical fifth-grade words. Eight Significant (SIG) errors at this level suggest an Instructional (INST) level. Seventeen Significant Word Recognition errors suggest that the student is Frustrated (FRUST) in Word Recognition at this level.[2] The same scoring rationale should be applied to the comprehension portion of the guide.

This guide is for the teacher to use in determining *realistic* independent and instructional levels. What if the student were to make three Significant Word Recognition errors? Or four? Does this indicate Independent or Instructional in decoding? The student's responses to words and questions must be evaluated by the teacher. Questions like these will be addressed in much greater depth in the next section: CRI INTERPRETATION. The scoring guide is just that—a guide. The teacher, not the guide, makes the final diagnosis.

---

[2] See pages 10–11 for a discussion of these levels.

Quick Reference for Abbreviations

- SIG WR = Significant Word Recognition
- COMP = Comprehension
- IND = Independent Level
- INST = Instructional Level
- FRUST = Frustration Level
- CRI = Classroom Reading Inventory
- (F) = Factual or Literal
- (I) = Inference
- (V) = Vocabulary

Summary of Specific Instructions

Step 1   Establish rapport. Don't be in a hurry to begin testing. Put the student at ease. Make him/her feel comfortable.

Step 2   Administer Part 1 Graded Word Lists. Always begin testing at the Preprimer Level.

Step 3   Administer Part 2 Graded Paragraphs. Begin at the highest level at which the student knew all twenty words in Part 1, Graded Word Lists.

Step 4   Background Knowledge Assessment. Before starting a graded paragraph, engage the student in a brief discussion about the story to be read. Attempt to uncover what the student knows about the topic, and try to get the student to make predictions about the story. If the student has some background knowledge, rate the student as *adequate*. If little or no background knowledge is evident, mark as *inadequate.*

Step 5   Graded Paragraphs. Have the student read the selection out loud. Make certain that the student understands that s/he will be asked to answer questions after each selection.

Step 6   Ask the questions, and be sure to record the student's responses if they differ from suggested responses.

Step 7   On the Graded Paragraphs, if the student reaches the frustration level in either word recognition or comprehension, or both, stop at that level.

Step 8   Complete the Inventory Record, and use the information garnered from the Graded Word Lists and the Graded Paragraphs to determine the estimated levels.

Step 9   Remember! It is the teacher that makes the final diagnosis (qualitative), not the number of errors recorded (quantitative).

CRI SCORING AND INTERPRETATION

Subskills Format
Form A: Pretest and Form A: Posttest

The Classroom Reading Inventory is designed to provide the teacher with a realistic estimate of the student's independent, instructional, frustration, and listening capacity levels in reading. However, merely identifying various reading levels is only slightly better than classifying the student on the basis of a norm-referenced test score.

The Classroom Reading Inventory is much more effective when the teacher is able to pinpoint consistent errors in word recognition or comprehension, or both. The Classroom Reading Inventory should enable the teacher to answer these specific questions.

- What is inhibiting fluent reading with comprehension? Is my student having difficulty recognizing the words (decoding function), or understanding the content (meaning function), or both?
- If the student's difficulty is in the area of word recognition, are there problems with consonants, vowels, or structure/syllables?
- If the student's difficulty is comprehension, are the problems with factual/literal questions, vocabulary questions, or inferential questions?
- Is the student a word caller, or a context reader?
- Does the student appear to have other needs? Does it appear that s/he needs glasses? Does the student appear to be anxious or withdrawn while reading aloud? Are high-interest/easy reading materials needed?

Following is a sample CRI record. This example is designed to help the teacher gain information on the scoring and interpretation of the CRI. Such information should enable the teacher to deal effectively with the types of questions presented previously.

Sample CRI Record—Deon

Deon is a fourth-grade student who is 9 years, 6 months old. His IQ, as measured by the Wechsler Intelligence Scale for Children–III, is in the average range. His grade equivalency in reading is 2.8, as measured by a group reading achievement test.

The score on the group reading achievement test is an indication that Deon's reading is below average for his grade level. The indication of below average reading, however, does not explain *why* Deon's reading is below average.

In order to determine why Deon's reading is not at grade level, Deon's teacher, Doris Cadd, administered Form A: Pretest of the CRI to Deon. His Inventory Record and Summary Sheet follow on pages 20 to 21.

> **Wherever you see this box on the following pages, go to www.classroom readinginventory.com to view the actual testing of Deon and Anna.**

Getting Started—Graded Word Lists:

Ms. Cadd: Deon, I have some words on these lists, and I want you to say them out loud for me. If you come to a word you don't know, it's OK to say—"I don't know." Just do the best you can.

Ms. Cadd then places the Form A: Pretest Preprimer-Primer (PP-P) Graded Word Lists in front of Deon, and pointing to the first word *this* on the preprimer list says, "OK, start here."

As Deon decodes the words on these lists, Ms. Cadd records his responses in the Inventory Record for Teachers, Form A. This procedure is followed with successive Graded Word Lists until the student misses five or more words in any column, at which point this part of the testing is stopped.

Ms. Cadd then moves on to the Graded Paragraphs.

Form A: Pretest Inventory Record
Summary Sheet

Student's Name: _____ Deon R. _____ Grade: ___4___ Age: __9-6__

year, months

Date: _10/17/08_ School: ____Robinson E.S.____ Administered by: ____Doris Cadd____

Part 1 Word Lists				Part 2 Graded Paragraphs		
Grade Level	Percentage of Words Correct	Word Recognition Errors		SIG WR	COMP	LC
		Consonants				
PP	100%	____consonants	PP	IND	IND	
		✓ blends				
P	90%	____digraphs	P	INST	IND	
		✓ endings				
1	80%	____compounds	1	INST	IND	
		____contractions				
2	70%		2	FRUST	IND	
		Vowels				
3	%	____long	3			100%
		✓ short				
		____long/short oo	4			80%
4	%	✓ vowel + r				
		____diphthong	5			40%
5	%	✓ vowel comb.				
		____a + l or w	6			
6	%		7			
		Syllable				
7	%	✓ visual patterns	8			
		✓ prefix				
8	%	✓ suffix				

Word Recognition Reinforcement and Vocabulary Development

Estimated Levels

	Grade
Independent	PP
Instructional	P–1 (range)
Frustration	2
Listening Capacity	4

Comp Errors
_____Factual (F)
_____Inference (I)
_____Vocabulary (V)
_____"Word Caller"
(A student who reads without associating meaning)
_____Poor Memory

Summary of Specific Needs:

Problems with phonetic and structural analysis. Needs help with short vowel sounds and irregular vowel combinations.

Form A: Pretest   **Part 1**   **Graded Word Lists**

PP			P			1			2	
1	this	✓	1	came	✓	1	new	*now*	1	birthday	✓
2	her	✓	2	day	✓	2	leg	✓	2	free	✓
3	about	✓	3	big	✓	3	feet	✓	3	isn't	✓
4	to	✓	4	house	✓	4	hear	*her*	4	beautiful	*boo-ful*
5	are	✓	5	after	✓	5	food	✓	5	job	✓
6	you	✓	6	how	✓	6	learn	✓	6	elephant	*P*
7	he	✓	7	put	✓	7	hat	✓	7	cowboy	✓
8	all	✓	8	other	*P*	8	ice	✓	8	branch	*beach*
9	like	✓	9	went	*want*	9	letter	✓	9	asleep	✓
10	could	✓	10	just	✓	10	green	✓	10	mice	✓
11	my	✓	11	play	✓	11	outside	✓	11	corn	✓
12	said	✓	12	many	✓	12	happy	✓	12	baseball	✓
13	was	✓	13	trees	✓	13	less	✓	13	garden	*grāden*
14	look	✓	14	boy	✓	14	drop	✓	14	hall	✓
15	go	✓	15	good	✓	15	stopping	(ing)	15	pet	✓
16	down	✓	16	girl	✓	16	grass	✓	16	blows	(s)
17	with	✓	17	see	✓	17	street	✓	17	gray	✓
18	what	✓	18	something	✓	18	page	✓	18	law	✓
19	been	✓	19	little	✓	19	ever	*even*	19	bat	✓
20	on	✓	20	saw	✓	20	let's	✓	20	guess	*gross*
		100%			*90%*			*80%*			*70%*

Teacher note: If the child misses five words in any column—stop Part 1. Begin Graded Paragraphs, Part 2 (Form A: Pretest), at the highest level in which the child recognized all 20 words. Each correct response equals 5%.

Scoring and Interpretation for Sample CRI—Deon

Part 1 Graded Words Lists—Scoring

- At the Preprimer (PP) Level, Deon decoded all twenty words correctly. Score = 100%.

- At the Primer (P) Level, Deon did not recognize word number 8 *other.* Therefore, Ms. Cadd pronounced the word *other* for Deon to maintain the flow and marked a *P* for *Pronounced.* Deon decoded *want* as *went,* and Ms. Cadd wrote *want* alongside the stimulus word *went.* Score = 90%.

- At Level 1 (first grade), Deon said *no* for *new, her* for *hear,* omitted the *ing* ending on *stopping,* and said *even* for *ever.* Score = 80%.

- At Level 2 (second grade), Deon decoded *beautiful* with a nonsense word *boo-ful.* He failed to decode *elephant* and Ms. Cadd pronounced it for him. Deon said *beach* for *branch,* decoded *garden* with a nonsense word *grāden,* omitted the *s* ending of the word *blows,* and said *gross* for *guess.* Score = 70%.

- Part 1 is now completed because Deon scored at 75% or below.

Part 1 Graded Word Lists—Interpretation

- For a fourth grader, Deon's phonetic and structural analysis skills are inadequate for his level of development. He appears to have particular difficulty with short vowel sounds and irregular vowel combinations such as *r* affected vowels and vowel digraphs. His basic sight word vocabulary also appears to be lacking.

- Let us now proceed to Part 2 Graded Paragraphs. Ms. Cadd will start Deon at the Preprimer (PP) Level as that's the level where Deon had all twenty words decoded correctly on Part 1 Graded Word Lists.

Web site www.classroomreadinginventory.com Reminder—Deon

Getting Started—Graded Paragraphs:

Ms. Cadd: Deon, on this part I have some stories that I want you to read out loud to me. After you finish a story, I will ask you some questions about what you read.

At this point, Ms. Cadd introduces the preprimer story "The Play Car" and completes the Background Knowledge Assessment by saying, "This story is about two children and a play car. Tell me what you think the children are doing."

Once the Background Knowledge Assessment has been completed, Ms. Cadd says, "Fine, Deon. Now, read this story out loud to me. It is called "The Play Car.""

When Deon finishes reading "The Play Car," Ms. Cadd removes the story from view and asks Deon the five questions.

This procedure is followed with successive stories until the student reaches the Frustration Level in word recognition and/or comprehension.

Form A: Pretest   Part 2/Level PP (38 Words)

Background Knowledge Assessment: This story is about two children and a play car. Tell me what you think the children are doing.

Adequate [✓]   Inadequate [   ]

THE PLAY CAR

Tom has a play car.

His play car is red.

"See my play car," said Tom.

"It can go fast."

Ann said, "It's a big car."

"I like your car."

"Good," said Tom.

"Would you like a ~~to~~ ride?"

Comprehension Check

(F) 1. ✓ What are the names of the boy and girl in this story?
(Tom and Ann)

(F) 2. ✓ What were they talking about?
(The play car)

(F) 3. ✓ Who owns the play car?
(Tom)

(F) 4. ✓ What color is the car?
(Red)

(I) 5. ✓ What do you think Tom likes about the car?
(It is big, fast)

Scoring Guide   Preprimer

SIG WR Errors		COMP Errors	
IND	0	IND	0–1
INST	2	INST	$1\frac{1}{2}$–2
FRUST	4+	FRUST	$2\frac{1}{2}$+

Background Knowledge Assessment: Has your class ever taken a field trip? Tell me about a field trip.

Adequate [✓]   Inadequate [ ]

OUR BUS RIDE

The children were all talking.

"No more talking, children," said Mrs. Brown.

"It is time for our trip."

"It is time to go to the farm."

Mrs. Brown said, "Get in the bus."

"Please do not push anyone."

riding
"We are ready to go now."

P
The children climbed into the bus.

Away went the bus.

the
It was a good day for a trip.

Comprehension Check

(F) 1. ___✓___ Where are they going?
(Farm)

(F) 2. ___✓___ How are they going?
(By bus)

(I) 3. ___✓___ Who do you think Mrs. Brown is?
(Teacher, bus driver, a parent)

(F) 4. ___✓___ How did the children know that it was time for the bus to leave?
(Mrs. Brown said, "We are ready to go now.") *Teacher told them*

(I) 5. ___✓___ Why do you think Mrs. Brown asked the children not to push anyone?
(Prevent accidents, any other reasonable answer)

Scoring Guide   Primer

SIG WR Errors		**COMP Errors**	
IND	0	(IND)	0–1
(INST)	3	INST	$1^1/_2$–2
FRUST	6+	FRUST	$2^1/_2$ +

Background Knowledge Assessment: This story is about puppies. What can you tell me about puppies?

Adequate [✓]   Inadequate [   ]

MARIA'S PUPPIES

Maria has two puppies.

She thinks that puppies are fun to ~~watch~~. *wash*

The puppies' names are *Sissy* and *Sassy*.

Puppies are ~~born~~ with their eyes closed. *brown*

Their ears are closed, too.

This is why they use their smell and touch.

After two weeks, puppies begin to open their

eyes and ears.

Most puppies can bark after four weeks.

Maria knows that *Sissy* and *Sassy* will grow up

~~to~~ be good pets. *and*

.

Comprehension Check

(F) 1. ___✓___   How many puppies does
                    Maria have?
                    (Two)

(F) 2. _1/2_   What are the puppies' names?
                    (Sissy and Sassy)   *Sissy and Sally*

(I) 3. __✓__   Why do you think that Maria
                    thinks puppies are fun to
                    watch?
                    (Any reasonable answer; e.g.,
                    they jump, roll around, chase
                    their tails)

(F) 4. __✓__   What can puppies do after
                    four weeks?
                    (Bark)

(F) 5. __✓__   At birth, puppies must use
                    their sense of smell and touch.
                    Why?
                    (Eyes or ears closed)

Scoring Guide   First

SIG WR Errors		COMP Errors	
~~IND~~	0	(IND)	0–1
(INST)	3	INST	1½–2
~~FRUST~~	6+	FRUST	2½+

Form A: Pretest   Part 2/Level 2 (76 Words)

Background Knowledge Assessment: What kinds of shows do you like to watch on TV?

Adequate ☑   Inadequate ☐

HOMEWORK FIRST

Marco and his sister Teresa love to ~~watch~~ *wash* TV.

The shows t~~hey~~ *that* like best are car̂toons.

Every day ~~after~~ *for* school they go (outside) to play.

Soon, Mother calls (to)them to come in.

"It's time to do your hômework," she says.

"When you f~~inish~~ *flash* your homework you can

watch your cartoons," Mother prômises.

"Remember! Homework first."

Marco and Teresa are happy with this.

They do their homework.

Now they are ready to watch ~~their~~ *the* cartoon

shows.

Comprehension Check

(F) 1. ___✓___   What do Marco and Teresa do first when they come home? (They go outside and play)

(F) 2. ___✓___   What did their mother promise them? (When they finish their homework they can watch cartoons [TV])

(V) 3. __DK__   What does *promise* mean? (To do what you say you will do; or any other reasonable answer)

(F) 4. ___✓___   What kinds of shows do Marco and Teresa like to watch the most? (Cartoons)

(I) 5. ___✓___   Other than cartoons, what shows do you think Marco and Teresa watch? (Any reasonable answer; e.g., movies, MTV, sports)

Scoring Guide   Second

SIG WR Errors		COMP Errors	
IND	2	(IND)	0–1
~~INST~~	4	INST	$1\frac{1}{2}$–2
(FRUST)	8+	FRUST	$2\frac{1}{2}$+

Form A: Pretest   Part 2/Level 3 (125 Words)

Background Knowledge Assessment: Have you ever been to Chicago? What do you know about Chicago?

Adequate ☑   Inadequate ☐

THE GREAT CHICAGO FIRE

It was early October of 1871. It was very dry in Chicago. Hardly any rain had fallen between July and October. Then on the evening of October 8, 1871, a fire started in the southwest side of the city.

It is believed the fire started in a barn owned by Mrs. Patrick O'Leary. A cow kicked over a lantern in the barn. There were strong winds that night. Flames raced north and east through the city. Many families fled north to Lincoln Park. Many other families raced into the cold waters of Lake Michigan. The fire wiped out the downtown area and most north side homes killing many people.

Chicago rose from the ruins of the fire to become one of the world's greatest cities.

Comprehension Check

(F) 1. ___✓___ How did the Chicago Fire start? (A cow kicked over a lantern in Mrs. O'Leary's barn)

(F) 2. ___✓___ Why was it so dry in Chicago when the fire started? (Very little rain had fallen that summer)

(V) 3. ___✓___ What is a *lantern*? (Like a lamp)

(I) 4. ___✓___ Why do you think many families fled to Lincoln Park? (Very little to burn in a park, or any other reasonable answer)

(F) 5. ___✓___ What month was it when the fire started? (October)

100%

Scoring Guide   Third

SIG WR Errors		COMP Errors	
IND	2	IND	0–1
INST	7	INST	$1^1/_2$–2
FRUST	14	FRUST	$2^1/_2$ +

Background Knowledge Assessment: Rosa Parks played a very important part in the Civil Rights Movement. What can you tell me about Rosa Parks or the Civil Rights Movement?

Adequate ☑   Inadequate ☐

TIRED OF GIVING IN

It was warm that December afternoon in Montgomery, Alabama. Rosa Parks was waiting for her city bus. She was tired from a long day of work—sewing.

When her bus came, Rosa took an empty seat in the "colored" section. In 1955, blacks could not sit in the front of the bus. However, they had to give up their seats in the middle to any white left standing.

Soon the front of the bus filled up. The white driver ordered Rosa to give up her seat to a white man. She didn't move. The driver called the police. Rosa was arrested.

Almost all of Montgomery's blacks, and some whites, staged a year-long boycott of the bus system to protest Rosa's arrest. The boycott was led by Martin Luther King, Jr. It ended when the Supreme Court ruled all bus segregation illegal.

Years later, Rosa Parks said, "I didn't give up my seat because I was tired. The only tired I was, was tired of giving in."

Comprehension Check

(F) 1. _✓_ Why was Rosa Parks arrested?
(She wouldn't give up her seat)

(V) 2. _✓_ What does the word *illegal* mean?
(Against the law, not legal)

(F) 3. _✓_ Who led the boycott of the bus system?
(Martin Luther King, Jr.)

(I) 4. _DK_ What do you think Rosa Parks meant when she said, "I was tired of giving in"?
(Any reasonable answer; e.g., she was tired of doing something that was not fair)

(I) 5. _✓_ Where do you think Rosa was going when she got on the bus?
(Any reasonable answer; e.g., home, to visit a friend)

80%

Scoring Guide   Fourth

SIG WR Errors		COMP Errors	
IND	3	IND	0–1
INST	8	INST	$1^1/_2$–2
FRUST	16	FRUST	$2^1/_2$ +

Background Knowledge Assessment: What do you know about pirates?

	Adequate	✓	Inadequate	

PIRATES!

Pirates were people who attacked and robbed ships. They raided towns like Charleston, South Carolina. Most people who became pirates hoped to get rich. Most pirates were men. A few women became pirates, too.

Movies have given us the idea that pirates led exciting lives. In real life, however, most pirates led miserable lives. Many pirates died of wounds or disease. Many were captured and hanged.

In the early 1700s, pirates sailed along the coast of South Carolina. They robbed ships sailing to or from Charleston. There were so many pirates around Charleston that few ships were safe.

One of these pirates was Stede Bonnet. Bonnet was very mean. He was the first pirate to make people "walk the plank."

William Rhett set out to capture Bonnet. He did, and took Bonnet and his crew to Charleston. All of Bonnet's crew were hanged. Just before Bonnet was to be hanged, a friend took him some women's clothes. Dressed as a woman, Bonnet was able to escape. Rhett went after him again. Bonnet was brought back to Charleston and hanged.

Pirates are gone now, but their stories live on.

Comprehension Check

(F) 1. —   How did Bonnet escape from jail? *He ran away*
(He dressed as a woman)

(F) 2. ✓   What happened to Bonnet?
(He was hanged)

(I) 3. ✓   Why do you think some women became pirates?
(Any reasonable answer; e.g., they wanted to get rich; they were married to pirates; they thought it would be exciting)

(V) 4. *DK*   What does the word *coast* mean in this story?
(Where the land meets the sea; the beach)

(I) 5. *DK*   What do you think *walk the plank* means?
(The pirates forced people to walk on a board until they fell overboard)

40%

Scoring Guide   Fifth

SIG WR Errors		**COMP Errors**	
IND	2	IND	0–1
INST	8	INST	$1\frac{1}{2}$–2
FRUST	17+	FRUST	$2\frac{1}{2}$+

Scoring and Interpretation for Sample CRI—Deon

Part 2 Graded Paragraphs—Scoring

Deon read aloud the Preprimer story. Because his only word recognition error (Deon said *to* for *a*) is a low-weighted (insignificant) error, Deon is considered to be independent for word recognition. Deon answered all of the questions correctly, so he is judged to be independent in comprehension.

In reading the Primer story, Deon made two significant word recognition errors. He said *riding* for *ready,* and Ms. Cadd had to pronounce *climbed* for him. In addition, there was one insignificant word recognition error. Deon said *the* for *a.* He is considered to be instructional for word recognition. Deon answered all of the questions correctly, so he is judged to be independent in comprehension.

Deon read the First Grade story and made two significant word recognition errors. He said *wash* for *watch,* and *brown* for *born.* Deon also made one insignificant word recognition error when he said *and* for *to.* Notice that in so doing he did not affect the meaning of the sentence. Deon answered four of the five questions correctly, and for one question he was given one-half credit because he miscalled one of the puppies' names. Deon is independent in comprehension.

From the number of significant word recognition errors Deon made with the Second Grade story, it is clear that he has reached frustration level with word recognition. His comprehension, however, continues to be at an independent level. At this point further oral reading of the graded paragraphs is discontinued.

Because Deon cannot decode successfully beyond a second-grade level, Ms. Cadd has decided to use the Listening Capacity Format in order to judge Deon's level of comprehension. Even with all of the decoding errors Deon made at the second-grade level, his comprehension is at the independent level.

Ms. Cadd decides to begin the Listening Capacity Format at the next highest level, the third-grade level.

Ms. Cadd: Deon, for these next stories, I will read the story out loud to you. You can follow the story as I read it. I will still ask you the questions at the end of the story. Be sure to pay close attention!

Ms. Cadd then places the Form A: Pretest Third Grade story, "Pony Express," in front of Deon while she reads the story to Deon from her copy. Upon completing the story, Ms. Cadd removes Deon's copy from view, and asks him the five questions.

This procedure is followed with successive stories until the student's level of comprehension falls below 70% on any given story.

Do not use the Scoring Guide for the Listening Capacity Format. Go to a numerical marking system instead. For example, a correct answer is worth 20 points, a one-half credit is worth 10 points, and no points for a wrong answer. Record the score after the last question.

With the Third Grade story comprehension was 100%, and 80% with the Fourth Grade story. With the Fifth Grade story comprehension dropped to 40%, which indicates inadequate comprehension at this level. No further testing of Deon is done.

Part 2 Graded Paragraphs—Interpretation

The results of Deon's testing on the CRI clearly indicate a problem with decoding. His phonetic and structural analysis skills are inadequate for his level of development. His comprehension, however, of stories he read, and stories read to him, was very good through a fourth-grade-reader level of difficulty. Deon is a **context reader.**

A **context reader** is a person whose phonetic and structural analysis skills are inadequate but who is still able to extract meaning from the context of the material despite the inadequate decoding skills.

In addition to this inventory of Deon's strengths and weaknesses, we also know that he is Independent in reading at a Preprimer level. Any reading that Deon is expected to do with no help from teacher or parent(s) should be at this level.

Deon is Instructional at a Primer/First Grade reading level. Use Primer level and early First Grade level material for purposes of instructing Deon in the decoding area.

Avoid having Deon do any reading at the Second Grade level as this is his level of Frustration, at least if he has to decode for himself.

Another way of looking at this discrepancy between Deon's level of decoding ability and his level of understanding is, for example, to take the word *cartoons*. Deon can say *cartoons* and he knows what the word *cartoons* means. He just doesn't know when he sees the word *cartoons* in print, that it's a word he knows, because he can't get it from print back into oral language where the meaning resides.

If the teacher can successfully remediate Deon's problems with decoding, Deon will be able to read at a Fourth Grade level because we know from the Listening Capacity test that he has good comprehension at that level.

Sample CRI Record—Anna

Anna is a third-grade student who is 8 years, 10 months old. Her IQ, as measured by the Wechsler Intelligence Scale for Children–III, is in the low average range. Her grade equivalency in reading is 1.5, as measured by a group reading achievement test.

The score on the group reading achievement test is an indication that Anna's reading is below average for her grade level. The indication of below average reading, however, does not explain *why* Anna's reading is below average.

In order to determine why Anna's reading is not at grade level, Anna's teacher, Liz Sage, administered Form A: Pretest of the CRI to Anna. Her Inventory Record and Summary Sheet follow on pages 32 to 34.

> **Web site www.classroomreadinginventory.com Reminder—Anna**

Getting Started—Graded Word Lists:

Ms. Sage: Anna, I have some words on these lists, and I want you to say them out loud for me. If you come to a word you don't know, it's OK to say, "I don't know." Just do the best you can.

Ms. Sage then places the Form A: Pretest Preprimer-Primer (PP-P) Graded Word Lists in front of Anna, and pointing to the first word *this* on the Preprimer list says, "OK Start here."

As Anna decodes the words on these lists, Ms. Sage records her responses in the Inventory Record for Teachers, Form A. This procedure is followed with successive Graded Word Lists until the student misses five or more words in any column, at which point this part of the testing is stopped. Ms. Sage then moves on to the Graded Paragraphs.

Form A: Pretest Inventory Record
Summary Sheet

Student's Name: _____Anna J._____ Grade: ___3___ Age: __8-10__
                                                          year, months

Date: _11/11/08_ School: ____Troost E.S._____ Administered by: ____Liz Sage____
_____

Part 1 Word Lists			Part 2 Graded Paragraphs			
Grade Level	**Percentage of Words Correct**	**Word Recognition Errors**		**SIG WR**	**COMP**	**LC**
		Consonants				
PP	100%	____consonants	PP			
		____blends				
P	100%	____digraphs	P	IND	IND	
		____endings				
1	95%	____compounds	1	IND	INST	
		____contractions				
2	95%		2	IND	FR	
		Vowels	3			
3	100%	____long				
		____short	4			
4	80%	____long/short oo				
		____vowel + r	5			
		____diphthong				
5	65%	____vowel comb.	6			
		____a + l or w				
6	___%		7			
		Syllable				
7	___%	____visual patterns	8			
		____prefix				
8	___%	____suffix				

Word Recognition Reinforcement and Vocabulary Development

Estimated Levels

	Grade
Independent	_P_
Instructional	_1_ (range)
Frustration	_2_
Listening Capacity	_N.D._

Comp Errors
- ✓ Factual (F)
- ✓ Inference (I)
- ✓ Vocabulary (V)
- ✓ "Word Caller" (A student who reads without associating meaning)
- ____ Poor Memory

Summary of Specific Needs:

Form A: Pretest　　　Part 1　　　Graded Word Lists

PP		**P**		**1**		**2**	
1 this	✓	1 came	✓	1 new	✓	1 birthday	✓
2 her	✓	2 day	✓	2 leg	✓	2 free	✓
3 about	✓	3 big	✓	3 feet	_foot_	3 isn't	✓
4 to	✓	4 house	✓	4 hear	✓	4 beautiful	✓
5 are	✓	5 after	✓	5 food	✓	5 job	✓
6 you	✓	6 how	✓	6 learn	✓	6 elephant	✓
7 he	✓	7 put	✓	7 hat	✓	7 cowboy	✓
8 all	✓	8 other	✓	8 ice	✓	8 branch	✓
9 like	✓	9 went	✓	9 letter	✓	9 asleep	✓
10 could	✓	10 just	✓	10 green	✓	10 mice	✓
11 my	✓	11 play	✓	11 outside	✓	11 corn	✓
12 said	✓	12 many	✓	12 happy	✓	12 baseball	✓
13 was	✓	13 trees	✓	13 less	✓	13 garden	✓
14 look	✓	14 boy	✓	14 drop	✓	14 hall	✓
15 go	✓	15 good	✓	15 stopping	✓	15 pet	✓
16 down	✓	16 girl	✓	16 grass	✓	16 blows	(5)
17 with	✓	17 see	✓	17 street	✓	17 gray	✓
18 what	✓	18 something	✓	18 page	✓	18 law	✓
19 been	✓	19 little	✓	19 ever	✓	19 bat	✓
20 on	✓	20 saw	✓	20 let's	✓	20 guess	✓
	_100%_		_100%_		_95%_		_95%_

Teacher note: If the child misses five words in any column—stop Part 1. Begin Graded Paragraphs, Part 2 (Form A: Pretest) at the highest level in which the child recognized all 20 words. Each correct response equals 5%.

3

1 distant ✓
2 phone ✓
3 turkeys ✓
4 bound ✓
5 chief ✓
6 foolish ✓
7 engage ✓
8 glow ✓
9 unhappy ✓
10 fully ✓
11 court ✓
12 energy ✓
13 passenger ✓
14 shark ✓
15 vacation ✓
16 pencil ✓
17 labor ✓
18 decided ✓
19 policy ✓
20 nail ✓

_100%_

4

1 drain ✓
2 jug ✓
3 innocent _P_
4 relax ✓
5 goodness ✓
6 seventeen ✓
7 disturb _dis-trub_
8 glove ✓
9 compass ✓
10 attractive ✓
11 impact ✓
12 lettuce ✓
13 operator ✓
14 regulation ✓
15 violet ✓
16 settlers ✓
17 polite _police_
18 internal _in-tern-nal_
19 drama ✓
20 landscape ✓

_80%_

5

1 moan _moon_
2 hymn _hum_
3 bravely ✓
4 instinct _instric_
5 shrill ✓
6 jewel ✓
7 onion ✓
8 register ✓
9 embarrass _P_
10 graceful ✓
11 cube _cub_
12 scar ✓
13 muffled ✓
14 pacing _passing_
15 oars ✓
16 guarantee ✓
17 thermometer ✓
18 zone ✓
19 salmon _sal-mon_
20 magical ✓

_65%_

6

1 brisk ____
2 nostrils ____
3 dispose ____
4 headlight ____
5 psychology ____
6 farthest ____
7 wreath ____
8 emptiness ____
9 billows ____
10 mob ____
11 biblical ____
12 harpoon ____
13 pounce ____
14 rumor ____
15 dazzle ____
16 combustion ____
17 hearth ____
18 mockingbird ____
19 ridiculous ____
20 widen ____

____%

Teacher note: If the child misses five words in any column—stop Part 1. Begin Graded Paragraphs, Part 2 (Form A: Pretest) at the highest level in which the child recognized all 20 words. Each correct response equals 5%.

Scoring and Interpretation for Sample CRI—Anna

Part 1 Graded Words Lists—Scoring

- At the Preprimer (PP) Level, Anna decoded all twenty words correctly. Score = 100%.

- At the Primer (P) Level, Anna decoded all twenty words correctly. Score = 100%.

- At Level 1 (first grade), Anna said *foot* for *feet*. Score = 95%.

- At Level 2 (second grade), Anna omitted the *s* ending of the word *blows*. Score = 95%.

- At Level 3 (third grade), Anna decoded all twenty words correctly. Score = 100%.

- At Level 4 (fourth grade), Anna did not recognize word number 3 *innocent*. Therefore, Ms. Sage pronounced the word *innocent* for Anna to maintain the flow and marked *P* for pronounced. Anna decoded *disturb* with a nonsense word *dis-trub,* said *police* for *polite,* and said *in-tern-nal* for *internal.* Score = 80%.

- At Level 5 (fifth grade), Anna said *moon* for *moan,* and *hum* for *hymn,* and decoded *instinct* with a nonsense word *instric.* She failed to decode *embarrass* and Ms. Sage pronounced it for her. Anna said *cub* for *cube, passing* for *pacing,* and *sal-mon* for *salmon.* Score = 65%.

- Part 1 is now completed because Anna scored at 65%.

Part 1 Graded Word Lists—Interpretation

- For a third grader, Anna's phonetic and structural analysis skills appear to be well established. Some of the words Anna miscued may be due to a lack of experience with a word with an irregular pronunciation; e.g., not knowing that the *l* in *salmon* is silent.

- Let us now proceed to Part 2 Graded Paragraphs. Ms. Sage will start Anna at the Primer (P) Level as that's the level where Anna had all twenty words decoded correctly on Part 1 Graded Word Lists.

Web site www.classroomreadinginventory.com Reminder—Anna

Getting Started—Graded Paragraphs:

Ms. Sage: Anna, on this next part I have some stories that I want you to read out loud to me. After you finish a story, I will ask you some questions about what you read.

At this point, Ms. Sage introduces the primer story "Our Bus Ride" and completes the Background Knowledge Assessment by saying, "Has your class ever taken a field trip? Tell me about a field trip."

Once the Background Knowledge Assessment has been completed, Ms. Sage says, "Fine, Anna. Now, read this story out loud to me. It is called "Our Bus Ride."

When Anna finishes reading "Our Bus Ride," Ms. Sage removes the story from view and asks Anna the five questions.

This procedure is followed with successive stories until the student reaches the Frustration Level in word recognition and/or comprehension.

Form A: Pretest   Part 2/Level P (62 Words)

Background Knowledge Assessment: Has your class ever taken a field trip? Tell me about a field trip.

Adequate [✓]   Inadequate [ ]

OUR BUS RIDE

The children were all talking.

"No more talking, children," said Mrs. Brown.

"It is time for our trip."

"It is time to go to the farm."

Mrs. Brown said, "Get ~~in~~ ^on^ the bus."

"Please do not push anyone."

"We are ready to go now."

The children climbed into the bus.

Away went the bus.

It was a good day for a trip.

Comprehension Check

(F) 1. __✓__ Where are they going?
(Farm)

(F) 2. __✓__ How are they going?
(By bus)

(I) 3. __✓__ Who do you think Mrs.
Brown is?
(Teacher, bus driver, a parent)

(F) 4. __✓__ How did the children know
that it was time for the bus to
leave?
(Mrs. Brown said, "We are
ready to go now.")

(I) 5. __D.K.__ Why do you think Mrs.
Brown asked the children not
to push anyone?
(Prevent accidents, any other
reasonable answer)

Scoring Guide   Primer

SIG WR Errors		**COMP Errors**	
(IND)	0	(IND)	0–1
INST	3	INST	$1\frac{1}{2}$–2
FRUST	6+	FRUST	$2\frac{1}{2}$+

Form A: Pretest   Part 2/Level 1 (71 Words)

Background Knowledge Assessment: This story is about puppies. What can you tell me about puppies?

Adequate [✓]   Inadequate [ ]

MARIA'S PUPPIES

Maria has two puppies.

She thinks that puppies are fun to watch.

The puppies' names are *Sissy* and *Sassy*.

Puppies are born with their eyes closed.

Their ears are closed, too.

This is why they use their smell and touch.

After two weeks, puppies begin to open their eyes and ears.

Most puppies can bark after four weeks.

Maria knows that *Sissy* and *Sassy* will grow up
and
~~to~~ be good pets.

.

Comprehension Check

(F) 1. ___✓___   How many puppies does Maria have?
(Two)

(F) 2. __¹/₂__   What are the puppies' names?
(Sissy and <u>Sassy</u>)

(I) 3. ___✓___   Why do you think that Maria thinks puppies are fun to watch?
(Any reasonable answer; e.g., they jump, roll around, chase their tails)

(F) 4. ___✓___   What can puppies do after four weeks?
(Bark)

(F) 5. _D.K._   At birth, puppies must use their sense of smell and touch. Why?
(Eyes or ears closed)

Scoring Guide   First

SIG WR Errors		COMP Errors	
(IND)	0	IND	0–1
INST	3	(INST)	1¹/₂–2
FRUST	6+	~~FRUST~~	2¹/₂+

Form A: Pretest   Part 2/Level 2 (76 Words)

Background Knowledge Assessment: What kinds of shows do you like to watch on TV?

Adequate [✓]   Inadequate [   ]

HOMEWORK FIRST

Marco and his sister Teresa love to watch TV.

The shows they like best are cartoons.

Every day after school they go outside ~~to~~ *and* play.

Soon, Mother calls to them to come in.

"It's time to do your homework," she says.

"When you finish your homework you can

watch your cartoons," Mother promises.

"Remember! Homework first."

Marco and Teresa are happy with this.

They do their homework.

Now they are ready to watch (their) cartoon

shows.

Comprehension Check

(F) 1. _____ What do Marco and Teresa do
first when they come home?
(They go outside and play)
homework

(F) 2. _✓_ What did their mother
promise them?
(When they finish their
homework they can watch
cartoons [TV])

(V) 3. _D.K._ What does *promise* mean?
(To do what you say you will
do; or any other reasonable
answer)

(F) 4. _✓_ What kinds of shows do
Marco and Teresa like to
watch the most?
(Cartoons)

(I) 5. _____ Other than cartoons, what
shows do you think Marco
and Teresa watch? *Scooby Doo*
(Any reasonable answer; e.g.,
movies, MTV, sports)

Scoring Guide   Second

SIG WR Errors		COMP Errors	
(IND)	2	IND	0–1
INST	4	INST	$1^1/_2$–2
FRUST	8+	(FRUST)	$2^1/_2$+

Scoring and Interpretation for Sample CRI—Anna

Part 2 Graded Paragraphs—Scoring

Anna read aloud the Primer story. Because her only word recognition error (Anna said *on* for *in*) is a low-weighted (insignificant) error, Anna is considered to be independent for word recognition. Anna answered all but one of the questions correctly, so she is judged to be independent in comprehension.

In reading the First Grade story, Anna made one insignificant word recognition error, she said *and* for *to.* She is considered to be independent for word recognition. Anna was able to recall only one of the puppies' names, so she received one-half credit. In addition, she was unable to answer question number 5, so she is judged to be instructional in comprehension.

Anna read the Second Grade story and made two low-weighted miscues, she said *and* for *to,* and omitted the word *their.* Anna is considered to be independent in word recognition. Anna missed three of the five questions, so she is judged to be at the frustration level in comprehension.

From the number of missed questions Anna made with the first- and second-grade stories, it is clear that she has reached frustration level with comprehension. No further testing is done.

Because Anna has reached the frustration level due to a problem with comprehension, the Listening Capacity Format is *not* used. The Listening Capacity Format is used only when a student's below average achievement in reading is due to a word recognition problem, and not a problem with comprehension.

Part 2 Graded Paragraphs—Interpretation

The results of Anna's testing on the CRI indicate a problem with comprehension. Anna appears to have difficulty with all areas of comprehension—factual/literal, vocabulary, and inferential/critical reading. Her phonetic and structural analysis skills, however, are well established for a third grader. Anna is a **word caller.** A **word caller** is a student whose decoding skills are well established but who does not assign meaning to what is decoded.

In addition to this inventory of Anna's strengths and weaknesses, we also know that she is Independent in reading at a Primer reading level. Any reading that Anna is expected to do with no help from teacher or parent(s) should be at this level.

Anna is instructional at a First Grade reading level. Use First Grade level material for purposes of instructing Anna in the comprehension area.

Avoid having Anna do any reading at the Second Grade level as this is her level of Frustration, at least if she has to associate meaning with what she reads.

SUBSKILLS FORMAT
FORM A: PRETEST

PART 1 Graded Word Lists

Form A: Pretest   Graded Word Lists

1	this		1	came
2	her		2	day
3	about		3	big
4	to		4	house
5	are		5	after
6	you		6	how
7	he		7	put
8	all		8	other
9	like		9	went
10	could		10	just
11	my		11	play
12	said		12	many
13	was		13	trees
14	look		14	boy
15	go		15	good
16	down		16	girl
17	with		17	see
18	what		18	something
19	bank		19	little
20	on		20	saw

Form A: Pretest   Graded Word Lists

1	new		1	birthday
2	leg		2	free
3	feet		3	isn't
4	hear		4	beautiful
5	food		5	job
6	learn		6	elephant
7	hat		7	cowboy
8	ice		8	branch
9	letter		9	asleep
10	green		10	mice
11	outside		11	corn
12	happy		12	baseball
13	less		13	garden
14	drop		14	hall
15	stopping		15	pet
16	grass		16	blows
17	street		17	gray
18	page		18	law
19	ever		19	bat
20	let's		20	guess

Form A: Pretest   Graded Word Lists

1	distant		1	drain
2	phone		2	jug
3	turkeys		3	innocent
4	bound		4	relax
5	chief		5	goodness
6	foolish		6	seventeen
7	engage		7	disturb
8	glow		8	glove
9	unhappy		9	compass
10	fully		10	attractive
11	court		11	impact
12	energy		12	lettuce
13	passenger		13	operator
14	shark		14	regulation
15	vacation		15	violet
16	pencil		16	settlers
17	labor		17	polite
18	decided		18	internal
19	policy		19	drama
20	nail		20	landscape

Form A: Pretest   Graded Word Lists

1	moan		1	brisk
2	hymn		2	nostrils
3	bravely		3	dispose
4	instinct		4	headlight
5	shrill		5	psychology
6	jewel		6	farthest
7	onion		7	wreath
8	register		8	emptiness
9	embarrass		9	billows
10	graceful		10	mob
11	cube		11	biblical
12	scar		12	harpoon
13	muffled		13	pounce
14	pacing		14	rumor
15	oars		15	dazzle
16	guarantee		16	combustion
17	thermometer		17	hearth
18	zone		18	mockingbird
19	salmon		19	ridiculous
20	magical		20	widen

Form A: Pretest   Graded Word Lists

1	proven		1	utilization
2	founder		2	valve
3	motivate		3	embodiment
4	glorify		4	kidnapper
5	adoption		5	offensive
6	popper		6	ghetto
7	nimble		7	profound
8	sanitation		8	discourse
9	unstable		9	impurity
10	dispatch		10	radiant
11	pompous		11	horrid
12	knapsack		12	vastly
13	bankruptcy		13	strenuous
14	geological		14	greedy
15	stockade		15	sanctuary
16	kerchief		16	quartet
17	glisten		17	tonal
18	obtainable		18	engender
19	pyramid		19	scallop
20	basin		20	gradient

SUBSKILLS FORMAT
FORM A: PRETEST

PART 2 Graded Paragraphs

THE PLAY CAR

Tom has a play car.

His play car is red.

"See my play car," said Tom.

"It can go fast."

Ann said, "It's a big car."

"I like your car."

"Good," said Tom.

"Would you like a ride?"

OUR BUS RIDE

The children were all talking.

"No more talking, children," said Mrs. Brown.

"It is time for our trip."

"It is time to go to the farm."

Mrs. Brown said, "Get in the bus."

"Please do not push anyone."

"We are ready to go now."

The children climbed into the bus.

Away went the bus.

It was a good day for a trip.

MARIA'S PUPPIES

Maria has two puppies.

She thinks that puppies are fun to watch.

The puppies' names are *Sissy* and *Sassy*.

Puppies are born with their eyes closed.

Their ears are closed, too.

This is why they use their smell and touch.

After two weeks, puppies begin to open their eyes and ears.

Most puppies can bark after four weeks.

Maria knows that *Sissy* and *Sassy* will grow up to be good pets.

HOMEWORK FIRST

Marco and his sister Teresa love to watch TV.

The shows they like best are cartoons.

Every day after school they go outside to play.

Soon, Mother calls to them to come in.

"It's time to do your homework," she says.

"When you finish your homework you can watch your cartoons," Mother promises.

"Remember! Homework first."

Marco and Teresa are happy with this.

They do their homework.

Now they are ready to watch their cartoon shows.

THE GREAT CHICAGO FIRE

It was early October of 1871. It was very dry in Chicago. Hardly any rain had fallen between July and October. Then on the evening of October 8, 1871, a fire started in the southwest side of the city.

It is believed the fire started in a barn owned by Mrs. Patrick O'Leary. A cow kicked over a lantern in the barn. There were strong winds that night. Flames raced north and east through the city. Many families fled north to Lincoln Park. Many other families raced into the cold waters of Lake Michigan. The fire wiped out the downtown area and most north side homes killing many people.

Chicago rose from the ruins of the fire to become one of the world's greatest cities.

TIRED OF GIVING IN

It was warm that December afternoon in Montgomery, Alabama. Rosa Parks was waiting for her city bus. She was tired from a long day of work—sewing.

When her bus came, Rosa took an empty seat in the "colored" section. In 1955, blacks could not sit in the front of the bus. However, they had to give up their seats in the middle to any white left standing.

Soon the front of the bus filled up. The white driver ordered Rosa to give up her seat to a white man. She didn't move. The driver called the police. Rosa was arrested.

Almost all of Montgomery's blacks, and some whites, staged a year-long boycott of the bus system to protest Rosa's arrest. The boycott was led by Martin Luther King, Jr. It ended when the Supreme Court ruled all bus segregation illegal.

Years later, Rosa Parks said, "I didn't give up my seat because I was tired. The only tired I was, was tired of giving in."

PIRATES!

Pirates were people who attacked and robbed ships. They raided towns like Charleston, South Carolina. Most people who became pirates hoped to get rich. Most pirates were men. A few women became pirates, too.

Movies have given us the idea that pirates led exciting lives. In real life, however, most pirates led miserable lives. Many pirates died of wounds or disease. Many were captured and hanged.

In the early 1700s, pirates sailed along the coast of South Carolina. They robbed ships sailing to or from Charleston. There were so many pirates around Charleston that few ships were safe.

One of these pirates was Stede Bonnet. Bonnet was very mean. He was the first pirate to make people "walk the plank."

William Rhett set out to capture Bonnet. He did, and took Bonnet and his crew to Charleston. All of Bonnet's crew were hanged. Just before Bonnet was to be hanged, a friend took him some women's clothes. Dressed as a woman, Bonnet was able to escape. Rhett went after him again. Bonnet was brought back to Charleston and hanged.

Pirates are gone now, but their stories live on.

BORN A SLAVE

He was born a slave on a farm in Missouri. When he was still a baby, his father was killed in an accident. His mother was kidnapped by night raiders. As a child, he was raised by Moses and Susan Carver. They were his owners. They named him George Washington Carver.

Mr. and Mrs. Carver taught George as a boy to read and write. He was very eager to learn, and showed a great interest in plants. When he was eleven years old he went to a school for black children in Neosho, Missouri.

For the next 20 years, Carver worked hard to pay for his education. George became a scientist and won worldwide fame for his agricultural research. He was widely praised for his work with peanuts. He made more than 300 things from peanuts. He also spent a great deal of time helping to improve race relations.

Carver got many awards for his work. The George Washington Carver National Monument was established on 210 acres of the Missouri farm where he was born.

THE OLD ONES

There is only one place in the United States where four states meet. It is the vast Four Corners region where Arizona, Colorado, New Mexico, and Utah come together.

The Four Corners region is a beautiful landscape of canyons, of flat mesas rising above broad valleys. It is slickrock desert and red dust and towering cliffs and the lonely sky.

About 2,000 years ago, a group of men and women the Navajo people call the *Anasazi* moved into this area. *Anasazi* is a Navajo word; it means "the Old Ones."

At first, the Anasazi dug out pits, and they lived in these "pit" houses. Later, they began to build houses out of stone and adobe called *pueblos*. They built their pueblos in and on the cliffs.

The Anasazi lived in these cliff houses for centuries. They farmed corn, raised children, created pottery, and traded with other pueblos.

Now these once great pueblos have been empty since the last years of the thirteenth century, for the Anasazi walked away from homes that had been theirs for 700 years.

Who were the Anasazi? Where did they come from? Where did they go? They simply left, and the entire Four Corners region lay silent, seemingly empty for 500 years.

YOUNG, GIFTED, AND BLACK

Lorraine Hansberry was the first black American playwright to achieve critical and popular success on Broadway.

Lorraine Hansberry was born in Chicago. In 1950 she moved to New York. In 1959 she became famous for her first completed play, *A Raisin in the Sun*. With this play, she won the Drama Critics Circle award.

A Raisin in the Sun is a play, a drama, about a black family's struggle to make a better life and to escape from a Chicago ghetto. It is a study of the search for identity by black men and women, both within the family and within a racially prejudiced American society.

She followed this moving and highly successful work with another play in 1964, *The Sign in Sidney Brustein's Window.*

Lorraine Hansberry's great promise was cut short by her death from cancer in 1965. Before her death at the age of 34, she began a play about race relations in Africa.

Selections from Hansberry's letters and works were published in *To Be Young, Gifted, and Black.*

SUBSKILLS FORMAT
FORM A: PRETEST

Inventory Record for Teachers

Form A: Pretest Inventory Record
Summary Sheet

Student's Name: _____ **Grade:** _____ **Age:** _____

year, months

Date: _____ **School:** _____ **Administered by:** _____

<table>
<tr>
<td colspan="3">Part 1
Word Lists</td>
<td colspan="4">Part 2
Graded Paragraphs</td>
</tr>
<tr>
<td>Grade Level</td>
<td>Percentage of Words Correct</td>
<td>Word Recognition Errors</td>
<td></td>
<td>SIG WR</td>
<td>COMP</td>
<td>LC</td>
</tr>
<tr>
<td>PP</td><td>_____ %</td>
<td>Consonants
_____ consonants
_____ blends</td>
<td>PP</td><td></td><td></td><td></td>
</tr>
<tr>
<td>P</td><td>_____ %</td>
<td>_____ digraphs
_____ endings</td>
<td>P</td><td></td><td></td><td></td>
</tr>
<tr>
<td>1</td><td>_____ %</td>
<td>_____ compounds
_____ contractions</td>
<td>1</td><td></td><td></td><td></td>
</tr>
<tr>
<td>2</td><td>_____ %</td>
<td></td>
<td>2</td><td></td><td></td><td></td>
</tr>
<tr>
<td>3</td><td>_____ %</td>
<td>Vowels
_____ long</td>
<td>3</td><td></td><td></td><td></td>
</tr>
<tr>
<td>4</td><td>_____ %</td>
<td>_____ short
_____ long/short oo</td>
<td>4</td><td></td><td></td><td></td>
</tr>
<tr>
<td>5</td><td>_____ %</td>
<td>_____ vowel + r
_____ diphthong</td>
<td>5</td><td></td><td></td><td></td>
</tr>
<tr>
<td>6</td><td>_____ %</td>
<td>_____ vowel comb.
_____ a + l or w</td>
<td>6</td><td></td><td></td><td></td>
</tr>
<tr>
<td>7</td><td>_____ %</td>
<td>Syllable</td>
<td>7</td><td></td><td></td><td></td>
</tr>
<tr>
<td>8</td><td>_____ %</td>
<td>_____ visual patterns
_____ prefix
_____ suffix

Word Recognition Reinforcement and Vocabulary Development</td>
<td>8</td><td></td><td></td><td></td>
</tr>
</table>

Estimated Levels   **Grade**

Independent   _____ /
Instructional   _____ / *(range)*
Frustration   _____ /
Listening Capacity   _____ /

Comp Errors
_____ Factual (F)
_____ Inference (I)
_____ Vocabulary (V)
_____ "Word Caller"
   (A student who reads without associating meaning)
_____ Poor Memory

Summary of Specific Needs:

Form A: Pretest   Part 1   Graded Word Lists

PP		P		1		2	
1 this	___	1 came	___	1 new	___	1 birthday	___
2 her	___	2 day	___	2 leg	___	2 free	___
3 about	___	3 big	___	3 feet	___	3 isn't	___
4 to	___	4 house	___	4 hear	___	4 beautiful	___
5 are	___	5 after	___	5 food	___	5 job	___
6 you	___	6 how	___	6 learn	___	6 elephant	___
7 he	___	7 put	___	7 hat	___	7 cowboy	___
8 all	___	8 other	___	8 ice	___	8 branch	___
9 like	___	9 went	___	9 letter	___	9 asleep	___
10 could	___	10 just	___	10 green	___	10 mice	___
11 my	___	11 play	___	11 outside	___	11 corn	___
12 said	___	12 many	___	12 happy	___	12 baseball	___
13 was	___	13 trees	___	13 less	___	13 garden	___
14 look	___	14 boy	___	14 drop	___	14 hall	___
15 go	___	15 good	___	15 stopping	___	15 pet	___
16 down	___	16 girl	___	16 grass	___	16 blows	___
17 with	___	17 see	___	17 street	___	17 gray	___
18 what	___	18 something	___	18 page	___	18 law	___
19 bank	___	19 little	___	19 ever	___	19 bat	___
20 on	___	20 saw	___	20 let's	___	20 guess	___
	___ %		___ %		___ %		___ %

Teacher note: If the child misses five words in any column—stop Part 1. Begin Graded Paragraphs, Part 2 (FORM A: Pretest), at the highest level in which the child recognized all 20 words. Each correct response equals 5%.

Form A: Pretest   **Part 1**   **Graded Word Lists**

3	4	5	6
1 distant ____	1 drain ____	1 moan ____	1 brisk ____
2 phone ____	2 jug ____	2 hymn ____	2 nostrils ____
3 turkeys ____	3 innocent ____	3 bravely ____	3 dispose ____
4 bound ____	4 relax ____	4 instinct ____	4 headlight ____
5 chief ____	5 goodness ____	5 shrill ____	5 psychology ____
6 foolish ____	6 seventeen ____	6 jewel ____	6 farthest ____
7 engage ____	7 disturb ____	7 onion ____	7 wreath ____
8 glow ____	8 glove ____	8 register ____	8 emptiness ____
9 unhappy ____	9 compass ____	9 embarrass ____	9 billows ____
10 fully ____	10 attractive ____	10 graceful ____	10 mob ____
11 court ____	11 impact ____	11 cube ____	11 biblical ____
12 energy ____	12 lettuce ____	12 scar ____	12 harpoon ____
13 passenger ____	13 operator ____	13 muffled ____	13 pounce ____
14 shark ____	14 regulation ____	14 pacing ____	14 rumor ____
15 vacation ____	15 violet ____	15 oars ____	15 dazzle ____
16 pencil ____	16 settlers ____	16 guarantee ____	16 combustion ____
17 labor ____	17 polite ____	17 thermometer ____	17 hearth ____
18 decided ____	18 internal ____	18 zone ____	18 mockingbird ____
19 policy ____	19 drama ____	19 salmon ____	19 ridiculous ____
20 nail ____	20 landscape ____	20 magical ____	20 widen ____
____ %	____ %	____ %	____ %

Teacher note: If the child misses five words in any column—stop Part 1. Begin Graded Paragraphs, Part 2 (FORM A: Pretest), at the highest level in which the child recognized all 20 words. Each correct response equals 5%.

Form A: Pretest   Graded Word Lists

7

1	proven	____
2	founder	____
3	motivate	____
4	glorify	____
5	adoption	____
6	popper	____
7	nimble	____
8	sanitation	____
9	unstable	____
10	dispatch	____
11	pompous	____
12	knapsack	____
13	bankruptcy	____
14	geological	____
15	stockade	____
16	kerchief	____
17	glisten	____
18	obtainable	____
19	pyramid	____
20	basin	____
		____ %

8

1	utilization	____
2	valve	____
3	embodiment	____
4	kidnapper	____
5	offensive	____
6	ghetto	____
7	profound	____
8	discourse	____
9	impurity	____
10	radiant	____
11	horrid	____
12	vastly	____
13	strenuous	____
14	greedy	____
15	sanctuary	____
16	quartet	____
17	tonal	____
18	engender	____
19	scallop	____
20	gradient	____
		____ %

Teacher note: If the child misses five words in any column—stop Part 1. Begin Graded Paragraphs, Part 2 (FORM A: Pretest), at the highest level in which the child recognized all 20 words. Each correct response equals 5%.

Form A: Pretest   Part 2/Level PP (38 Words)

Background Knowledge Assessment: This story is about two children and a play car. Tell me what you think the children are doing.

Adequate ☐   Inadequate ☐

THE PLAY CAR

Tom has a play car.

His play car is red.

"See my play car," said Tom.

"It can go fast."

Ann said, "It's a big car."

"I like your car."

"Good," said Tom.

"Would you like a ride?"

Comprehension Check

(F) 1. _____ What are the names of the boy and girl in this story?
(Tom and Ann)

(F) 2. _____ What were they talking about?
(The play car)

(F) 3. _____ Who owns the play car?
(Tom)

(F) 4. _____ What color is the car?
(Red)

(I) 5. _____ What do you think Tom likes about the car?
(It is big, fast)

Scoring Guide   Preprimer

SIG WR Errors		COMP Errors	
IND	0	IND	0–1
INST	2	INST	$1^{1}/_{2}$–2
FRUST	4+	FRUST	$2^{1}/_{2}$+

Form A: Pretest   Part 2/Level P (62 Words)

Background Knowledge Assessment: Has your class ever taken a field trip? Tell me about a field trip.

Adequate [   ]   Inadequate [   ]

OUR BUS RIDE

The children were all talking.

"No more talking, children," said Mrs. Brown.

"It is time for our trip."

"It is time to go to the farm."

Mrs. Brown said, "Get in the bus."

"Please do not push anyone."

"We are ready to go now."

The children climbed into the bus.

Away went the bus.

It was a good day for a trip.

Comprehension Check

(F) 1. _____ Where are they going?
(Farm)

(F) 2. _____ How are they going?
(By bus)

(I) 3. _____ Who do you think Mrs. Brown is?
(Teacher, bus driver, a parent)

(F) 4. _____ How did the children know that it was time for the bus to leave?
(Mrs. Brown said, "We are ready to go now.")

(I) 5. _____ Why do you think Mrs. Brown asked the children not to push anyone?
(Prevent accidents, any other reasonable answer)

Scoring Guide   Primer

SIG WR Errors		COMP Errors	
IND	0	IND	0–1
INST	3	INST	$1\frac{1}{2}$–2
FRUST	6+	FRUST	$2\frac{1}{2}$+

Form A: Pretest   Part 2/Level 1 (71 Words)

Background Knowledge Assessment: This story is about puppies. What can you tell me about puppies?

Adequate [   ]   Inadequate [   ]

MARIA'S PUPPIES

Maria has two puppies.

She thinks that puppies are fun to watch.

The puppies' names are *Sissy* and *Sassy*.

Puppies are born with their eyes closed.

Their ears are closed, too.

This is why they use their smell and touch.

After two weeks, puppies begin to open their

eyes and ears.

Most puppies can bark after four weeks.

Maria knows that *Sissy* and *Sassy* will grow up

to be good pets.

.

Comprehension Check

(F) 1. _____ How many puppies does Maria have? (Two)

(F) 2. _____ What are the puppies' names? (Sissy and Sassy)

(I) 3. _____ Why do you think that Maria thinks puppies are fun to watch? (Any reasonable answer; e.g., they jump, roll around, chase their tails)

(F) 4. _____ What can puppies do after four weeks? (Bark)

(F) 5. _____ At birth, puppies must use their sense of smell and touch. Why? (Eyes or ears closed)

Scoring Guide   First

SIG WR Errors		COMP Errors	
IND	0	IND	0–1
INST	3	INST	$1\frac{1}{2}$–2
FRUST	6+	FRUST	$2\frac{1}{2}$+

Background Knowledge Assessment: What kinds of shows do you like to watch on TV?

Adequate ☐   Inadequate ☐

HOMEWORK FIRST

Marco and his sister Teresa love to watch TV.

The shows they like best are cartoons.

Every day after school they go outside to play.

Soon, Mother calls to them to come in.

"It's time to do your homework," she says.

"When you finish your homework you can

watch your cartoons," Mother promises.

"Remember! Homework first."

Marco and Teresa are happy with this.

They do their homework.

Now they are ready to watch their cartoon

shows.

Comprehension Check

(F) 1. _____ What do Marco and Teresa do first when they come home? (They go outside and play)

(F) 2. _____ What did their mother promise them? (When they finish their homework they can watch cartoons [TV])

(V) 3. _____ What does *promise* mean? (To do what you say you will do; or any other reasonable answer)

(F) 4. _____ What kinds of shows do Marco and Teresa like to watch the most? (Cartoons)

(I) 5. _____ Other than cartoons, what shows do you think Marco and Teresa watch? (Any reasonable answer; e.g., movies, MTV, sports)

Scoring Guide   Second

SIG WR Errors		COMP Errors	
IND	2	IND	0–1
INST	4	INST	$1\frac{1}{2}$–2
FRUST	8+	FRUST	$2\frac{1}{2}$+

Form A: Pretest   Part 2/Level 3 (125 Words)

Background Knowledge Assessment: Have you ever been to Chicago? What do you know about Chicago?

Adequate ☐   Inadequate ☐

THE GREAT CHICAGO FIRE

It was early October of 1871. It was very dry in Chicago. Hardly any rain had fallen between July and October. Then on the evening of October 8, 1871, a fire started in the southwest side of the city.

It is believed the fire started in a barn owned by Mrs. Patrick O'Leary. A cow kicked over a lantern in the barn. There were strong winds that night. Flames raced north and east through the city. Many families fled north to Lincoln Park. Many other families raced into the cold waters of Lake Michigan. The fire wiped out the downtown area and most north side homes killing many people.

Chicago rose from the ruins of the fire to become one of the world's greatest cities.

Comprehension Check

(F) 1. _____ How did the Chicago Fire start? (A cow kicked over a lantern in Mrs. O'Leary's barn)

(F) 2. _____ Why was it so dry in Chicago when the fire started? (Very little rain had fallen that summer)

(V) 3. _____ What is a *lantern*? (Like a lamp)

(I) 4. _____ Why do you think many families fled to Lincoln Park? (Very little to burn in a park, or any other reasonable answer)

(F) 5. _____ What month was it when the fire started? (October)

Scoring Guide   Third

SIG WR Errors		COMP Errors	
IND	2	IND	0–1
INST	7	INST	$1^1/_2$–2
FRUST	14	FRUST	$2^1/_2$+

Form A: Pretest   Part 2/Level 4 (166 Words)

Background Knowledge Assessment: Rosa Parks played a very important part in the Civil Rights Movement. What can you tell me about Rosa Parks or the Civil Rights Movement?

Adequate ☐   Inadequate ☐

TIRED OF GIVING IN

It was warm that December afternoon in Montgomery, Alabama. Rosa Parks was waiting for her city bus. She was tired from a long day of work—sewing.

When her bus came, Rosa took an empty seat in the "colored" section. In 1955, blacks could not sit in the front of the bus. However, they had to give up their seats in the middle to any white left standing.

Soon the front of the bus filled up. The white driver ordered Rosa to give up her seat to a white man. She didn't move. The driver called the police. Rosa was arrested.

Almost all of Montgomery's blacks, and some whites, staged a year-long boycott of the bus system to protest Rosa's arrest. The boycott was led by Martin Luther King, Jr. It ended when the Supreme Court ruled all bus segregation illegal.

Years later, Rosa Parks said, "I didn't give up my seat because I was tired. The only tired I was, was tired of giving in."

Comprehension Check

(F) 1. _____   Why was Rosa Parks arrested?
(She wouldn't give up her seat)

(V) 2. _____   What does the word *illegal* mean?
(Against the law, not legal)

(F) 3. _____   Who led the boycott of the bus system?
(Martin Luther King, Jr.)

(I) 4. _____   What do you think Rosa Parks meant when she said, "I was tired of giving in"?
(Any reasonable answer; e.g., she was tired of doing something that was not fair)

(I) 5. _____   Where do you think Rosa was going when she got on the bus?
(Any reasonable answer; e.g., home, to visit a friend)

Scoring Guide   Fourth

SIG WR Errors		COMP Errors	
IND	3	IND	0–1
INST	8	INST	$1^1/_2$–2
FRUST	16	FRUST	$2^1/_2$ +

Form A: Pretest   Part 2/Level 5 (158 Words)

Background Knowledge Assessment: What do you know about pirates?

PIRATES!

Pirates were people who attacked and robbed ships. They raided towns like Charleston, South Carolina. Most people who became pirates hoped to get rich. Most pirates were men. A few women became pirates, too.

Movies have given us the idea that pirates led exciting lives. In real life, however, most pirates led miserable lives. Many pirates died of wounds or disease. Many were captured and hanged.

In the early 1700s, pirates sailed along the coast of South Carolina. They robbed ships sailing to or from Charleston. There were so many pirates around Charleston that few ships were safe.

One of these pirates was Stede Bonnet. Bonnet was very mean. He was the first pirate to make people "walk the plank."

William Rhett set out to capture Bonnet. He did, and took Bonnet and his crew to Charleston. All of Bonnet's crew were hanged. Just before Bonnet was to be hanged, a friend took him some women's clothes. Dressed as a woman, Bonnet was able to escape. Rhett went after him again. Bonnet was brought back to Charleston and hanged.

Pirates are gone now, but their stories live on.

Adequate   Inadequate

☐   ☐

Comprehension Check

(F) 1. _____   How did Bonnet escape from jail?
(He dressed as a woman)

(F) 2. _____   What happened to Bonnet?
(He was hanged)

(I) 3. _____   Why do you think some women become pirates?
(Any reasonable answer; e.g., they wanted to get rich; they were married to pirates; they thought it would be exciting)

(V) 4. _____   What does the word *coast* mean in this story?
(Where the land meets the sea; the beach)

(I) 5. _____   What do you think *walk the plank* means?
(The pirates forced people to walk on a board until they fell overboard)

Scoring Guide   Fifth

SIG WR Errors		COMP Errors	
IND	2	IND	0–1
INST	8	INST	$1^{1}/_{2}$–2
FRUST	17+	FRUST	$2^{1}/_{2}$+

Form A: Pretest   Part 2/Level 6 (175 Words)

Background Knowledge Assessment: Had you heard about George Washington Carver before reading the story? What do you remember about him?

BORN A SLAVE

He was born a slave on a farm in Missouri. When he was still a baby, his father was killed in an accident. His mother was kidnapped by night raiders. As a child, he was raised by Moses and Susan Carver. They were his owners. They named him George Washington Carver.

Mr. and Mrs. Carver taught George as a boy to read and write. He was very eager to learn, and showed a great interest in plants. When he was eleven years old he went to a school for black children in Neosho, Missouri.

For the next 20 years, Carver worked hard to pay for his education. George became a scientist and won worldwide fame for his agricultural research. He was widely praised for his work with peanuts. He made more than 300 things from peanuts. He also spent a great deal of time helping to improve race relations.

Carver got many awards for his work. The George Washington Carver National Monument was established on 210 acres of the Missouri farm where he was born.

Adequate   Inadequate

☐   ☐

Comprehension Check

(F) 1. _____ Where was George Washington Carver born? (Missouri)

(F) 2. _____ What did George become? (Scientist)

(I) 3. _____ Why do you think George became so interested in plants? (He grew up on a farm. or any other reasonable answer)

(V) 4. _____ What does the word *improve* mean? (To make something better)

(F) 5. _____ What was the plant that Carver worked most with? (The peanut)

Scoring Guide   Sixth

SIG WR Errors		COMP Errors	
IND	2	IND	0–1
INST	8	INST	$1\frac{1}{2}$–2
FRUST	17+	FRUST	$2\frac{1}{2}$+

Form A: Pretest   Part 2/Level 7 (207 Words)

Background Knowledge Assessment: This story is about some Native Americans called the Anasazi. The Anasazi once lived in the southwestern United States. What can you tell me about Native American Indians?

THE OLD ONES

There is only one place in the United States where four states meet. It is the vast Four Corners region where Arizona, Colorado, New Mexico, and Utah come together.

The Four Corners region is a beautiful landscape of canyons, of flat mesas rising above broad valleys. It is slickrock desert and red dust and towering cliffs and the lonely sky.

About 2,000 years ago, a group of men and women the Navajo people call the *Anasazi* moved into this area. *Anasazi* is a Navajo word; it means "the Old Ones."

At first, the Anasazi dug out pits, and they lived in these "pit" houses. Later, they began to build houses out of stone and adobe called *pueblos*. They built their pueblos in and on the cliffs.

The Anasazi lived in these cliff houses for centuries. They farmed corn, raised children, created pottery, and traded with other pueblos.

Now these once great pueblos have been empty since the last years of the thirteenth century, for the Anasazi walked away from homes that had been theirs for 700 years.

Who were the Anasazi? Where did they come from? Where did they go? They simply left, and the entire Four Corners region lay silent, seemingly empty for 500 years.

Adequate	Inadequate
☐	☐

Comprehension Check

(F) 1. _____ Name two of the states in the Four Corners region.
(Arizona, Colorado, New Mexico, or Utah)

(V) 2. _____ What is a *century*?
(100 years)

(I) 3. _____ Why do you think Navajo named these people "The Old Ones"?
(Because they were the people who lived there long before the Navajo did; or any other reasonable explanation)

(I) 4. _____ What do you think caused the Anasazi to leave their homes?
(Any reasonable explanation; e.g., bad weather, war, some natural disaster)

(F) 5. _____ How long ago was it when the Anasazi moved into the Four Corners region?
(About 2,000 years ago)

Scoring Guide   Seventh

SIG WR Errors		COMP Errors	
IND	2	IND	0–1
INST	11	INST	$1^1/_2$–2
FRUST	22+	FRUST	$2^1/_2$+

Background Knowledge Assessment: This story tells about a famous playwright. Playwrights write plays. Tell me about a play you know.

YOUNG, GIFTED, AND BLACK

Lorraine Hansberry was the first black American playwright to achieve critical and popular success on Broadway.

Lorraine Hansberry was born in Chicago. In 1950 she moved to New York. In 1959 she became famous for her first completed play, *A Raisin in the Sun*. With this play, she won the Drama Critics Circle award.

A Raisin in the Sun is a play, a drama, about a black family's struggle to make a better life and to escape from a Chicago ghetto. It is a study of the search for identity by black men and women, both within the family and within a racially prejudiced American society.

She followed this moving and highly successful work with another play in 1964, *The Sign in Sidney Brustein's Window*.

Lorraine Hansberry's great promise was cut short by her death from cancer in 1965. Before her death at the age of 34, she began a play about race relations in Africa.

Selections from Hansberry's letters and works were published in *To Be Young, Gifted, and Black*.

Adequate   Inadequate

☐   ☐

Comprehension Check

(V) 1. _____ What does *highly* successful mean in this story? (Very successful; it was a great success)

(F) 2. _____ Where was Lorraine Hansberry born? (Chicago)

(F) 3. _____ In *A Raisin in the Sun*, what was the family trying to escape from? (A Chicago ghetto; a bad neighborhood)

(I) 4. _____ What do you think would have happened to Lorraine Hansberry if she hadn't died young? (Any reasonable answer; e.g., kept writing plays/dramas)

(F) 5. _____ What caused Lorraine's death? (Cancer)

Scoring Guide   Eighth

SIG WR Errors		COMP Errors	
IND	2	IND	0–1
INST	8	INST	$1^1/_2$–2
FRUST	17+	FRUST	$2^1/_2$ +

SUBSKILLS FORMAT
FORM A: POSTTEST

PART 1 Graded Word Lists

Form A: Posttest   Graded Word Lists

1	in		1	three
2	now		2	find
3	so		3	because
4	from		4	head
5	get		5	their
6	had		6	before
7	at		7	more
8	over		8	turn
9	of		9	think
10	into		10	call
11	no		11	these
12	came		12	school
13	but		13	word
14	has		14	even
15	if		15	would
16	as		16	ask
17	have		17	much
18	be		18	want
19	or		19	never
20	an		20	your

Form A: Posttest   Graded Word Lists

1	maybe		1	sound
2	pass		2	climb
3	out		3	waiting
4	they		4	hands
5	please		5	cry
6	love		6	doctor
7	cannot		7	people
8	eight		8	everyone
9	kind		9	strong
10	read		10	inch
11	paid		11	rock
12	open		12	sea
13	top		13	thirty
14	pool		14	dance
15	low		15	test
16	late		16	hard
17	giant		17	dogs
18	short		18	story
19	upon		19	city
20	us		20	push

Form A: Posttest   Graded Word Lists

1	computer		1	spy
2	angry		2	downtown
3	energy		3	tray
4	choice		4	lung
5	hospital		5	exhibit
6	court		6	formal
7	heard		7	weekend
8	closet		8	nineteen
9	meet		9	mixture
10	picnic		10	invitation
11	against		11	happiness
12	law		12	gulf
13	build		13	rumble
14	objects		14	plot
15	probably		15	tennis
16	shot		16	weary
17	we'll		17	lantern
18	paragraph		18	preparation
19	telephone		19	weep
20	sugar		20	jelly

Form A: Posttest   Graded Word Lists

1	sensation		1	radiant
2	analyze		2	greatness
3	funeral		3	tardy
4	scissors		4	doughnut
5	mutual		5	armor
6	consistent		6	nurture
7	deliberately		7	dismay
8	officially		8	shipment
9	taxi		9	logic
10	parachute		10	pulley
11	radar		11	fingerprint
12	intermediate		12	jumbo
13	embarrass		13	guppy
14	raid		14	narrator
15	crude		15	crutch
16	bakery		16	shopper
17	knelt		17	punish
18	endure		18	silken
19	painful		19	omelet
20	squash		20	miniature

Form A: Posttest Graded Word Lists

1	noisily		1	duly
2	imperative		2	furnishing
3	forge		3	emptiness
4	expressway		4	frustration
5	nominate		5	joyously
6	include		6	patriotic
7	formulate		7	zeal
8	enact		8	seriousness
9	depot		9	notorious
10	illegal		10	federation
11	distress		11	youth
12	childish		12	selection
13	unfair		13	bleak
14	sentimental		14	mutton
15	designer		15	habitation
16	luggage		16	fling
17	historically		17	dungeon
18	uncertainty		18	hierarchy
19	gardener		19	duration
20	enchant		20	journalist

SUBSKILLS FORMAT
FORM A: POSTTEST

PART 2 Graded Paragraphs

FISHING

Bob and Pam went fishing.

Bob put his line in the water.

He felt something pull on his line.

"A fish! A fish!" said Bob.

"Help me get it, Pam."

Pam said, "It's a big one."

Bob said, "We can get it."

JOSE'S FIRST AIRPLANE RIDE

Jose and his papa went to the airport.

Jose was very happy.

His papa was happy, too.

They got on the airplane.

Up high into the sky they flew.

"How high we are," said Jose.

"The cars look so small."

"And so do the houses," said Papa.

Jose said, "This is so much fun."

PLANT SPIDERS

There are all kinds of spiders.

Some spiders are big, and some spiders are small.

One kind of spider is called a plant spider.

Plant spiders are black and green in color.

Plant spiders have eight legs.

All spiders have eight legs.

Plant spiders spin their webs on plants.

That is why they are called plant spiders.

They soon learn to hunt for food and spin thcir wcbs.

THE RODEO

It is a warm, sunny day. Many people have come to the rodeo to see Bob Hill ride Midnight. Bob Hill is one of the best cowboys in the rodeo. Midnight is one of the best horses in the rodeo. He is big and fast. Midnight is a strong black horse.

The people at the rodeo stood up. They are all waiting for the big ride. Can Bob Hill ride the great horse Midnight?

GREAT WALL OF CHINA

The Chinese began work on the Great Wall about 2,000 years ago. Over time, it became the largest wall ever built. The Great Wall is about 25 feet high with watch-towers used for lookout posts. The Great Wall is almost 4,000 miles long. It was built to keep China safe from invaders from the north.

For the most part, the Great Wall kept China safe from these enemies. However, the armies of the Mongol leader Genghis Khan did cross the wall 900 years ago and conquered most of China.

Today, the Chinese no longer use the wall for defense. Visitors from all over the world come to see the Great Wall and walk the path along its top.

The Great Wall of China is the only man-made structure that can be seen by the astronauts as they orbit the earth.

THE RED KNIGHT OF GERMANY

Baron Manfred von Richthofen was known as the Red Baron or the Red Knight. *Baron* is a noble title meaning "warrior" among the early Germans. This baron was a warrior in the sky and the top ace of World War I.

An ace is an airplane pilot who shoots down at least five enemy aircraft during a war. The planes must either crash or be forced to land. During World War I, the leading aces were thought of as great heroes. They were seen as daring knights of the air.

The Red Baron shot down 80 enemy planes. He became known as the Red Knight because his plane was painted bright red. He would come flashing out of the sun. With his machine guns blazing, he forced many enemy planes to crash before their pilots knew what was happening. A plane shot down is known as a kill.

The Red Baron's streak of 80 kills came to an end when a little-known Canadian pilot, Roy Brown, shot down the Red Knight of Germany.

ZEPPELIN

It was the evening of May 6, 1937. Rain had been falling that day. The place was Lakehurst, New Jersey. More than 1,000 people had come to Lakehurst to see the airship of the future. They had come to see the great German zeppelin *Hindenburg* end a flight from Europe to the United States.

"There she is!" someone shouted. A great silver shape came out of the mist and light rain. In just a few minutes the *Hindenburg* would be ready to be tied to the mooring mast.

Two landing lines dropped down from the ship. At exactly 7:23, fire burst from the tail of the great zeppelin. The ship seemed to blow apart. In just 30 seconds, the world's greatest zeppelin lay black, broken, and smoking on Lakehurst field.

The burning of the *Hindenburg* spelled the end for the zeppelin. No more were ever built. What was supposed to be the "ship of the future" became a dead thing of the past.

ALONG THE OREGON TRAIL

Today Missouri is in the central part of the United States. In 1800, it was not the center. In those days Missouri was on the edge of the frontier. Very few people had ever seen the great lands that lay to the west of Missouri. In 1804, Captain Meriwether Lewis and William Clark set out from St. Louis to explore these lands. In November 1805, they reached the Pacific Ocean. The route they took later became known as the Oregon Trail. When they returned, Lewis and Clark told many exciting stories about the West. This made other people want to make the West their home. By the 1830s, settlers began making the long trip to the West. Missouri was the starting place for almost all these settlers. In Independence, St. Joseph, or Westport, they bought wagons, tools, and food for the two-thousand-mile trip. They went along the Oregon Trail through plains and deserts, over mountains, and across rivers.

TITANIC

The *Titanic* was the largest ship in the world. The *Titanic* was thought to be unsinkable.

On the night of April 14, 1912, the sea was calm, and the night was clear and cold. The *Titanic* was on its first trip from England to New York. The captain had received warnings of icebergs ahead. He decided to keep going at full speed and keep a sharp watch for any icebergs.

The men on watch aboard *Titanic* saw an iceberg just ahead. It was too late to avoid it. The iceberg tore a 300-foot gash in the *Titanic's* side. The ship sank in about 2½ hours.

Of the 2,200 passengers and crew, only 705 people were saved. They were mostly women and children.

In 1985, researchers from France and the United States found the *Titanic* at the bottom of the Atlantic Ocean. Sharks and other fish now swam along the decaying decks where joyful passengers once strolled.

THE DIARY

Anne Frank, a young Jewish girl, was born in Germany in 1929. A few years after Anne's birth, Adolf Hitler and the Nazi party came to power in Germany. Germany was in a great economic depression at the time, and Hitler blamed these problems on the Jews. To escape the persecution of the Nazis, Anne and her family, like many other Jews, fled to Holland. There in Amsterdam, Anne grew up in the 1930s and early 1940s.

For her thirteenth birthday, Anne received a diary. She began writing in it. In 1942, Hitler conquered Holland, and the Nazis soon began rounding up the Jews to send them to concentration camps. Millions of Jews died in these camps.

To escape the Nazis, the Franks went into hiding. Some of their Dutch friends hid Anne and her family in some secret rooms above a warehouse in Amsterdam. In that small space the Franks lived secretly for more than two years. During that time, Anne continued to write in her diary.

By the summer of 1944, World War II was coming to an end. The American and British armies freed Holland from the Nazis, but not in time to save Anne and her family. Police discovered their hiding place and sent Anne and her family to concentration camps. Anne Frank died in the camp at Bergen-Belsen in March 1945. She was not yet sixteen years old.

All of the Franks died in the camps except Anne's father. After the war, Mr. Frank returned to Amsterdam. He revisited the small, secret rooms his family had hidden in for so long. Among the trash and broken furniture, he found Anne's diary.

SUBSKILLS FORMAT
FORM A: POSTTEST

Inventory Record for Teachers

Form A: Posttest Inventory Record
Summary Sheet

Student's Name: _____ Grade: _____ Age: _____

year, months

Date: _____ School: _____ Administered by: _____

Part 1 Word Lists			Part 2 Graded Paragraphs			

Grade Level	Percentage of Words Correct	Word Recognition Errors		SIG WR	COMP	LC
		Consonants				
PP	____ %	____ consonants	PP			
		____ blends				
P	____ %	____ digraphs	P			
		____ endings				
1	____ %	____ compounds	1			
		____ contractions				
2	____ %		2			
		Vowels				
3	____ %	____ long	3			
		____ short				
4	____ %	____ long/short oo	4			
		____ vowel + r				
5	____ %	____ diphthong	5			
		____ vowel comb.				
6	____ %	____ a + l or w	6			
			7			
7	____ %	**Syllable**				
		____ visual patterns	8			
8	____ %	____ prefix				
		____ suffix				

Word Recognition Reinforcement and Vocabulary Development

Estimated Levels	Grade
Independent	____ /
Instructional	____ / (range)
Frustration	____ /
Listening Capacity	____ /

Comp Errors
____ Factual (F)
____ Inference (I)
____ Vocabulary (V)
____ "Word Caller"
(A student who reads without
associating meaning)
____ Poor Memory

Summary of Specific Needs:

Form A: Posttest   Part 1   Graded Word Lists

PP		P		1		2	
1 in	___	1 three	___	1 maybe	___	1 sound	___
2 now	___	2 find	___	2 pass	___	2 climb	___
3 so	___	3 because	___	3 out	___	3 waiting	___
4 from	___	4 head	___	4 they	___	4 hands	___
5 get	___	5 their	___	5 please	___	5 cry	___
6 had	___	6 before	___	6 love	___	6 doctor	___
7 at	___	7 more	___	7 cannot	___	7 people	___
8 over	___	8 turn	___	8 eight	___	8 everyone	___
9 of	___	9 think	___	9 kind	___	9 strong	___
10 into	___	10 call	___	10 read	___	10 inch	___
11 no	___	11 these	___	11 paid	___	11 rock	___
12 came	___	12 school	___	12 open	___	12 sea	___
13 but	___	13 word	___	13 top	___	13 thirty	___
14 has	___	14 even	___	14 pool	___	14 dance	___
15 if	___	15 would	___	15 low	___	15 test	___
16 as	___	16 ask	___	16 late	___	16 hard	___
17 have	___	17 much	___	17 giant	___	17 dogs	___
18 be	___	18 want	___	18 short	___	18 story	___
19 or	___	19 never	___	19 upon	___	19 city	___
20 an	___	20 your	___	20 us	___	20 push	___
	___ %		___ %		___ %		___ %

Teacher note: If the child misses five words in any column—stop Part 1. Begin Graded Paragraphs, Part 2 (FORM A: Posttest), at the highest level in which the child recognized all 20 words. Each correct response equals 5%.

Form A: Posttest   **Part 1**   **Graded Word Lists**

3	4	5	6
1 computer ___	1 spy ___	1 sensation ___	1 radiant ___
2 angry ___	2 downtown ___	2 analyze ___	2 greatness ___
3 energy ___	3 tray ___	3 funeral ___	3 tardy ___
4 choice ___	4 lung ___	4 scissors ___	4 doughnut ___
5 hospital ___	5 exhibit ___	5 mutual ___	5 armor ___
6 court ___	6 formal ___	6 consistent ___	6 nurture ___
7 heard ___	7 weekend ___	7 deliberately ___	7 dismay ___
8 closet ___	8 nineteen ___	8 officially ___	8 shipment ___
9 meet ___	9 mixture ___	9 taxi ___	9 logic ___
10 picnic ___	10 invitation ___	10 parachute ___	10 pulley ___
11 against ___	11 happiness ___	11 radar ___	11 fingerprint ___
12 law ___	12 gulf ___	12 intermediate___	12 jumbo ___
13 build ___	13 rumble ___	13 embarrass ___	13 guppy ___
14 objects ___	14 plot ___	14 raid ___	14 narrator ___
15 probably ___	15 tennis ___	15 crude ___	15 crutch ___
16 shot ___	16 weary ___	16 bakery ___	16 shopper ___
17 we'll ___	17 lantern ___	17 knelt ___	17 punish ___
18 paragraph ___	18 preparation ___	18 endure ___	18 silken ___
19 telephone ___	19 weep ___	19 painful ___	19 omelet ___
20 sugar ___	20 jelly ___	20 squash ___	20 miniature ___
___ %	___ %	___ %	___ %

Teacher note: If the child misses five words in any column—stop Part 1. Begin Graded Paragraphs, Part 2 (FORM A: Posttest), at the highest level in which the child recognized all 20 words. Each correct response equals 5%.

Form A: Posttest   Graded Word Lists

7

1	noisily	_____
2	imperative	_____
3	forge	_____
4	expressway	_____
5	nominate	_____
6	include	_____
7	formulate	_____
8	enact	_____
9	depot	_____
10	illegal	_____
11	distress	_____
12	childish	_____
13	unfair	_____
14	sentimental	_____
15	designer	_____
16	luggage	_____
17	historically	_____
18	uncertainty	_____
19	gardener	_____
20	enchant	_____
	_____ %	

8

1	duly	_____
2	furnishing	_____
3	emptiness	_____
4	frustration	_____
5	joyously	_____
6	patriotic	_____
7	zeal	_____
8	seriousness	_____
9	notorious	_____
10	federation	_____
11	youth	_____
12	selection	_____
13	bleak	_____
14	mutton	_____
15	habitation	_____
16	fling	_____
17	dungeon	_____
18	hierarchy	_____
19	duration	_____
20	journalist	_____
	_____ %	

Teacher note: If the child misses five words in any column—stop Part 1. Begin Graded Paragraphs, Part 2 (FORM A: Posttest), at the highest level in which the child recognized all 20 words. Each correct response equals 5%.

Form A: Posttest   Part 2/Level PP (43 Words)

Background Knowledge Assessment: This story is about two children who went fishing. Have you ever gone fishing? Tell me about it.

Adequate ☐   Inadequate ☐

FISHING

Bob and Pam went fishing.

Bob put his line in the water.

He felt something pull on his line.

"A fish! A fish!" said Bob.

"Help me get it, Pam."

Pam said, "It's a big one."

Bob said, "We can get it."

Comprehension Check

(F) 1. _____ What are the names of the boy and girl in this story?
(Bob and Pam)

(F) 2. _____ What were they doing?
(Fishing)

(F) 3. _____ What did Bob feel pull on his line?
(A fish)

(F) 4. _____ What did Pam say?
(It's a big one, a big fish)

(I) 5. _____ What do you think Bob and Pam did with the fish?
(Any reasonable answer; e.g., cooked it, let it go)

Scoring Guide   Preprimer

SIG WR Errors		**COMP Errors**	
IND	0	IND	0–1
INST	2	INST	$1^1/_2$–2
FRUST	4+	FRUST	$2^1/_2$ +

Background Knowledge Assessment: Have you ever flown in an airplane? Tell me about it. If not, tell me what you think it might be like.

Adequate ☐　　　Inadequate ☐

JOSE'S FIRST AIRPLANE RIDE

Comprehension Check

Jose and his papa went to the airport.

Jose was very happy.

His papa was happy, too.

They got on the airplane.

Up high into the sky they flew.

"How high we are," said Jose.

"The cars look so small."

"And so do the houses," said Papa.

Jose said, "This is so much fun."

(F) 1. _____ Who is with Jose on the airplane? (Father, Papa)

(F) 2. _____ What words in the story told you that Jose liked his ride? (*Jose was very happy*; *This is so much fun*)

(V) 3. _____ What does the word *high* mean in this story? (Way up in the air, above the houses and cars)

(I) 4. _____ Why do you think Jose's papa took him for an airplane ride? (Any reasonable answer; e.g., because he had not been on an airplane before; they went to visit relatives)

(F) 5. _____ How many airplane rides did Jose have before this one? (None)

Scoring Guide　　　Primer

SIG WR Errors		COMP Errors	
IND	0	IND	0–1
INST	2	INST	$1\frac{1}{2}$–2
FRUST	5+	FRUST	$2\frac{1}{2}$+

Form A: Posttest Part 2/Level 1 (68 Words)

Background Knowledge Assessment: This story is about spiders. What can you tell me about spiders?

Adequate [   ]   Inadequate [   ]

PLANT SPIDERS

There are all kinds of spiders.

Some spiders are big, and some spiders are

small.

One kind of spider is called a plant spider.

Plant spiders are black and green in color.

Plant spiders have eight legs.

All spiders have eight legs.

Plant spiders spin their webs on plants.

That is why they are called plant spiders.

They soon learn to hunt for food and spin

their webs.

Comprehension Check

(F) 1. _____ Are there more than one kind of spider?
(Yes—many more)

(F) 2. _____ What color is the spider in this story?
(Black and green)

(V) 3. _____ What does the word *plant* mean in this story?
(Student gives an example of a plant)

(I) 4. _____ What do you think spiders eat?
(Flies, bugs, insects)

(F) 5. _____ How many legs do all spiders have?
(Eight)

Scoring Guide   First

SIG WR Errors		COMP Errors	
IND	0	IND	0–1
INST	3	INST	$1\frac{1}{2}$–2
FRUST	6+	FRUST	$2\frac{1}{2}$+

Background Knowledge Assessment: Have you ever been to a rodeo or seen one on TV? What do you know about rodeos?

Adequate ☐   Inadequate ☐

THE RODEO

It was a warm, sunny day. Many people had come to the rodeo to see Bob Hill ride Midnight. Bob Hill is one of the best cowboys in the rodeo. Midnight is one of the best horses in the rodeo. He is big and fast. Midnight is a strong black horse.

The people at the rodeo stood up. They were all waiting for the big ride. Can Bob Hill ride the great horse Midnight?

Comprehension Check

(F)   1. _____ What was the weather like on the day of the rodeo? (Warm and sunny)

(I)   2. _____ The people seemed to be excited. Why? (They wanted to see this great horse and/or cowboy)

(F)   3. _____ What was the name of the horse? (Midnight)

(F)   4. _____ What did he (Midnight) look like? (Big, fast, strong, black)

(I)   5. _____ Why do you think that Bob Hill was a good rider? (Story said he was one of the best cowboys in the rodeo)

Scoring Guide   Second

SIG WR Errors		**COMP Errors**	
IND	0	IND	0–1
INST	3	INST	$1\frac{1}{2}$–2
FRUST	7+	FRUST	$2\frac{1}{2}$+

Form A: Posttest **Part 2/Level 3 (140 Words)**

Background Knowledge Assessment: What do you know about China and/or the Great Wall of China?

Adequate ☐   Inadequate ☐

GREAT WALL OF CHINA

The Chinese began work on the Great Wall about 2,000 years ago. Over time, it became the largest wall ever built. The Great Wall is about 25 feet high with watchtowers used for lookout posts. The Great Wall is almost 4,000 miles long. It was built to keep China safe from invaders from the north.

For the most part, the Great Wall kept China safe from these enemies. However, the armies of the Mongol leader Genghis Khan did cross the wall 900 years ago and conquered most of China.

Today, the Chinese no longer use the wall for defense. Visitors from all over the world come to see the Great Wall and walk the path along its top.

The Great Wall of China is the only man-made structure that can be seen by the astronauts as they orbit the earth.

Comprehension Check

(F) 1. _____ Why was the Great Wall of China built? (To protect China from its enemies)

(F) 2. _____ How long is the Great Wall? (About 4,000 miles long)

(I) 3. _____ Would you go to China to see the Great Wall? Why or why not? (Any reasonable answer)

(V) 4. _____ What does the word *defense* mean? (Protection, to protect someone or something)

(F) 5. _____ Who was Genghis Khan? (The Mongol leader, the man who crossed the wall)

Scoring Guide   Third

SIG WR Errors		**COMP Errors**	
IND	1	IND	0–1
INST	7	INST	$1^1/_2$–2
FRUST	15+	FRUST	$2^1/_2$+

Background Knowledge Assessment: What do you know about World War I?

Adequate [   ]   Inadequate [   ]

THE RED KNIGHT OF GERMANY

Comprehension Check

Baron Manfred von Richthofen was known as the Red Baron or the Red Knight. *Baron* is a noble title meaning "warrior" among the early Germans. This baron was a warrior in the sky and the top ace of World War I.

An ace is an airplane pilot who shoots down at least five enemy aircraft during a war. The planes must either crash or be forced to land. During World War I, the leading aces were thought of as great heroes. They were seen as daring knights of the air.

The Red Baron shot down 80 enemy planes. He became known as the Red Knight because his plane was painter bright red. He would come flashing out of the sun. With his machine guns blazing, he forced many enemy planes to crash before their pilots knew what was happening. A plane shot down is known as a kill

The Red Baron's streak of 80 kills came to an end when a little known-Canadian pilot, Roy Brown, shot down the Red Knight of Germany.

(F) 1. _____ Why was von Richthofen known as the Red Knight or Red Baron? (His plane was painted a bright red)

(F) 2. _____ How many kills did the Red Baron have? (80)

(V) 3. _____ What is a *hero*? (A person who does something brave, or any other reasonable answer)

(I) 4. _____ Why do you think the Red Baron was so great a pilot? (He took chances, he was very daring, or any other reasonable answer)

(F) 5. _____ Who was Roy Brown? (The pilot who shot down Baron von Richthofen)

Scoring Guide   Fourth

SIG WR Errors		**COMP Errors**	
IND	2	IND	0–1
INST	6	INST	$1^1/_2$–2
FRUST	12+	FRUST	$2^1/_2$+

Form A: Posttest   Part 2/Level 5 (156 Words)

Background Knowledge Assessment: A zeppelin, sometimes called a dirigible, is like a blimp. You see blimps flying over sporting events. Tell me about blimps.

Adequate ☐   Inadequate ☐

ZEPPELIN

It was the evening of May 6, 1937. Rain had been falling that day. The place was Lakehurst, New Jersey. More than 1,000 people had come to Lakehurst to see the airship of the future. They had come to see the great German zeppelin *Hindenburg* end a flight from Europe to the United States.

"There she is!" someone shouted. A great silver shape came out of the mist and light rain. In just a few minutes the *Hindenburg* would be ready to be tied to the mooring mast.

Two landing lines dropped down from the ship. At exactly 7:23, fire burst from the tail of the great zeppelin. The ship seemed to blow apart. In just 30 seconds, the world's greatest zeppelin lay black, broken, and smoking on Lakehurst field.

The burning of the *Hindenburg* spelled the end for the zeppelin. No more were ever built. What was supposed to be the "ship of the future" became a dead thing of the past.

Comprehension Check

(F) 1. _____ What was the weather like when the *Hindenburg* tried to land?
(It was raining, it was misty)

(F) 2. _____ Where was the *Hindenburg* coming from when it tried to land at Lakehurst?
(Europe)

(V) 3. _____ What does the word *silver* mean in this story?
(It is the color of the airship)

(I) 4. _____ What do you think caused the *Hindenburg* to catch fire?
(Any reasonable explanation; e.g., a short circuit, lightning)

(I) 5. _____ Why do you think no more zeppelins were ever built?
(Any reasonable explanation; e.g., they were unsafe)

Scoring Guide   Fifth

SIG WR Errors		COMP Errors	
IND	2	IND	0–1
INST	7	INST	$1^1/_2$–2
FRUST	15+	FRUST	$2^1/_2$+

Form A: Posttest   Part 2/Level 6 (163 Words)

Background Knowledge Assessment: Two famous American explorers were Lewis and Clark. What do you know about them?

Adequate [   ]   Inadequate [   ]

ALONG THE OREGON TRAIL

Today Missouri is in the central part of the United States. In 1800, it was not the center. In those days Missouri was on the edge of the frontier. Very few people had ever seen the great lands that lay to the west of Missouri. In 1804, Captain Meriwether Lewis and William Clark set out from St. Louis to explore these lands. In November 1805, they reached the Pacific Ocean. The route they took later became known as the Oregon Trail. When they returned, Lewis and Clark told many exciting stories about the West. This made other people want to make the West their home. By the 1830s, settlers began making the long trip to the West. Missouri was the starting place for almost all these settlers. In Independence, St. Joseph, or Westport, they bought wagons, tools, and food for the two-thousand-mile trip. They went along the Oregon Trail through plains and deserts, over mountains, and across rivers.

Comprehension Check

(F) 1. _____ From what city did Lewis and Clark set out to explore the West?
(St. Louis)

(F) 2. _____ At the end of their long journey, what ocean did they reach?
(Pacific Ocean)

(V) 3. _____ What is a *trail*?
(Path, road, like a street)

(I) 4. _____ Why do you think people wanted to make the long trip West?
(So they could have more land; they heard exciting stories about the West; or any other reasonable explanation)

(F) 5. _____ In what state are the cities of Independence and St. Joseph?
(Missouri)

Scoring Guide   Sixth

SIG WR Errors		COMP Errors	
IND	2	IND	0–1
INST	8	INST	$1^1/_2$–2
FRUST	16+	FRUST	$2^1/_2$+

Form A: Posttest   Part 2/Level 7 (159 Words)

Background Knowledge Assessment: The *Titanic* is probably the most famous ship in the world. What can you tell me about the *Titanic?*

Adequate ☐ Inadequate ☐

TITANIC

The *Titanic* was the largest ship in the world. The *Titanic* was thought to be unsinkable.

On the night of April 14, 1912, the sea was calm, and the night was clear and cold. The *Titanic* was on its first trip from England to New York. The captain had received warnings of icebergs ahead. He decided to keep going at full speed and keep a sharp watch for any icebergs.

The men on watch aboard *Titanic* saw an iceberg just ahead. It was too late to avoid it. The iceberg tore a 300-foot gash in the *Titanic's* side. The ship sank in about $2\frac{1}{2}$ hours.

Of the 2,200 passengers and crew, only 705 people were saved. They were mostly women and children.

In 1985, researchers from France and the United States found the *Titanic* at the bottom of the Atlantic Ocean. Sharks and other fish now swam along the decaying decks where joyful passengers once strolled.

Comprehension Check

(V) 1. _____ What is an *iceberg?*
(It's like a mountain of ice; a huge pile of ice)

(F) 2. _____ What was the weather like on the night the *Titanic* sank?
(It was clear and cold)

(V) 3. _____ What does it mean to keep a *sharp watch?*
(To look for something very carefully; to be on the lookout for something)

(I) 4. _____ If you had the chance, would you want to go down and see the *Titanic?* Why or why not?
(Any reasonable explanation)

(F) 5. _____ Where was the *Titanic* going when it left England?
(New York)

Scoring Guide   Seventh

SIG WR Errors		COMP Errors	
IND	2	IND	0–1
INST	8	INST	$1\frac{1}{2}$–2
FRUST	15+	FRUST	$2\frac{1}{2}$+

Background Knowledge Assessment: Many people were killed by the Nazis during World War II. Perhaps one of the most famous was a young Jewish girl named Anne Frank. What do you know about Anne?

Adequate [ ] Inadequate [ ]

THE DIARY

Anne Frank, a young Jewish girl, was born in Germany in 1929. A few years after Anne's birth, Adolf Hitler and the Nazi party came to power in Germany. Germany was in a great economic depression at the time, and Hitler blamed these problems on the Jews. To escape the persecution of the Nazis, Anne and her family, like many other Jews, fled to Holland. There in Amsterdam, Anne grew up in the 1930s and early 1940s.

For her thirteenth birthday, Anne received a diary. She began writing in it. In 1942, Hitler conquered Holland, and the Nazis soon began rounding up the Jews to send them to concentration camps. Millions of Jews died in these camps.

To escape the Nazis, the Franks went into hiding. Some of their Dutch friends hid Anne and her family in some secret rooms above a warehouse in Amsterdam. In that small space the Franks lived secretly for more than two years. During that time, Anne continued to write in her diary.

By the summer of 1944, World War II was coming to an end. The American and British armies freed Holland from the Nazis, but not in time to save Anne and her family. Police discovered their hiding place and sent Anne and her family to concentration camps. Anne Frank died in the camp at Bergen-Belsen in March 1945. She was not yet sixteen years old.

All of the Franks died in the camps except Anne's father. After the war, Mr. Frank returned to Amsterdam. He revisited the small, secret rooms his family had hidden in for so long. Among the trash and broken furniture, he found Anne's diary.

Comprehension Check

(V) 1. _____ What does the word *persecution* mean? (To cause harm, suffering or death; to hunt down; to pursue)

(F) 2. _____ Who found Anne's diary? (Her father)

(F) 3. _____ Why did Anne and her family go into hiding? (To escape the Nazis)

(I) 4. _____ What do you think Anne wrote about in her diary? (Any reasonable answer; e.g., what it is like to be in hiding)

(I) 5. _____ How do you think the Nazis discovered the Franks' hiding place? (Someone told on them; the police searched all the buildings; or any other reasonable answer)

Scoring Guide	Eighth		
SIG WR Errors		**COMP Errors**	
IND	3	IND	0–1
INST	11	INST	$1\frac{1}{2}$–2
FRUST	26+	FRUST	$2\frac{1}{2}$+

USING THE CRI:
SPECIFIC INSTRUCTIONS

For Administering the Reader Response Format
Form B: Pretest and Form B: Posttest

Introduction

The READER RESPONSE FORMAT is based on the following five assumptions. First, the essential factors involved in *reading comprehension* are prior knowledge and prior experience. Second, individual reader responses are affected by the reader's prior knowledge and experience. Third, the reader uses language (reader responses) to organize and reconstruct his or her prior knowledge and experience. Fourth, the reader is able to express prior knowledge and experience by making **Predictions** and **Retelling** the story, in his or her own words. And, finally, it is believed that it is possible to assess the reader's ability to predict and retell and thereby gain valuable insights into the reader's ability to comprehend story material.

Thus, Form B: Reader Response Format is designed around the **Predicting** and **Retelling** of stories and divides these two essential factors into the following four scorable parts:

Student Ability	Scorable Parts
Predicting	1. *Predicting*—the use of the title to anticipate story or selection contents.
Retelling	2. *Character(s)*—the use of character(s) to deal with essential elements.
	3. *Problem(s)*—those elements used by the character(s) in the story to identify problem(s) or reach goal(s).
	4. *Outcome(s)*—usually deals with how the character(s) solved the problem(s) or attained the goal(s).

Prompting and Comfortable Reading Level

Prompting

To help assess a student's reading ability, teachers must become familiar with the concept of prompting. Teachers need to know how to prompt, when to prompt, and how much to prompt.

EXAMPLE: Let's say you ask a student to define the word *hat*. The answer you are looking for is "a hat is something you wear on your head." The student's reply, however, is "a hat is something you wear." This is not a complete answer so you prompt in a *general* way so as not to suggest the answer you want. You say to the student: "Tell me more about a hat." The student replies: "A hat is made of cloth." Still not the answer you are after. Now you prompt in a more *suggestive* way by saying: "Where do you wear a hat?" The student answers: "You wear a hat when you go outside." At this point the prompt becomes *specific* and you say: "Yes, but on what part of your body do you wear a hat?" How much prompting does it take to arrive at the answer you deem necessary to indicate understanding on the student's part?

There are times when the teacher will guide the student by prompting. There are times when prompting is not necessary, and the teacher will not interrupt the free flow of reader response.

Reading Level

As the teacher listens to the student read and later discuss the story, is the student Independent (IND), Instructional (INST), or Frustration (FRUST) at a given grade level? What is meant by Independent, Instructional, and Frustration?

- *Independent:* The oral reading of the story is fluent and expressive; there are few, if any, significant word recognition errors. During the retelling, the student has no difficulty in recalling the character(s), or the problem(s) and the outcome(s)/solution(s). This is the student's independent level.
- *Instructional:* The oral reading of the selection is somewhat hesitant with an attempt at fluency; there are indications of an increasing number of significant word recognition errors. During the retelling, the student exhibits some difficulty in recalling the character(s), or the problem(s) and outcome(s)/solution(s). The teacher finds it necessary to do some *general* prompting. This is the student's instructional level.
- *Frustration:* The oral reading of the story is word-by-word and with much hesitation; there are a significant number of word recognition errors. During the retelling, even with *suggestive* and *specific* prompting, the student is not able to tell you much about the story. This is the student's frustration level.

Preparing Students for Individual Evaluation

Traditionally, reading instruction has required students to read a selection and then to answer questions as a way of developing and assessing comprehension. It seems reasonable to assume that the ability to make predictions and retell the story are usually not taught in most traditional reading programs. If this is true, and your students are in a traditional reading program, the teacher should either (a) use Form A: Subskills Format or (b) teach students how to predict and retell before administering Form B: Reader Response Format.

In most reading programs, reading evaluation tends to occur near the beginning of the school year. Therefore, it is recommended that before administering Form B: Reader Response Pretests and Posttests the teacher needs to model the predicting and retelling procedure with the whole class or with small groups.

What follows is a discussion of how to prepare students to make predictions and to retell stories in their own words. This will be followed by an example of how the teacher might actually model the procedure for students. It is believed that after the discussion and illustration of how to model the procedure for students, the teacher will be able to use Form B: Reader Response Pre-Post Testing for individual students.

Classroom Environment for Predicting and Retelling

Some students might not become involved easily in making predictions and retelling stories, even after the teacher models the procedure. If students are not sure of what to say or do, teachers may need to base their lessons on student experiences and social activities. The teacher should emphasize that a student's willingness to try is of utmost importance.

The teacher should consider the following:

- Develop themes or topics based on the age and interests of students; e.g., young students: animals or pets; older students: TV shows.
- Use a variety of instructional groupings: small groups, whole class, or pairs.
- During this preparation period, students will need similar copies of stories and titles.
- During the predicting part, have students use only the title.

Steps in Predicting and Retelling Preparation Period

Predicting: (Allow approximately five minutes for predicting.)

Step 1   Use the title and ask the students to predict the plot or problem. Initially, ask them to work in pairs. Each pair of students can elect to write or discuss their responses. If they do write their responses, do not collect the papers.

Step 2   Ask the students to report their predictions. Record the predictions on the chalkboard, and discuss them. Predictions might be about plot, problem, or words in the title. Tell students they will come back to their predictions after they have had an opportunity to hear the selection read by the teacher and have read it themselves.

Retelling: (Allow approximately ten minutes for retelling.)

Step 3   The students are to follow the selection as the teacher reads it aloud. After the teacher completes the selection, s/he should ask the students to read the selection silently. Again, it is more important for the student to understand the selection than it is for the student to memorize the selection.

Step 4   Go back to step one and discuss the various student predictions, not on the basis of whether they are correct or incorrect (good or bad) responses but rather on how "close" the predictions were or the "fun" of making predictions.

The previous steps merely outline the procedures used during prediction and retelling. What follows is an example of how to **introduce** these procedures in a lesson where the teacher is asked to **model** them for students.

Teacher as Model

Find a simple selection. The selection should have a title. The title must be large enough to be seen by the students.

Show the title. The teacher might make several predictions about what s/he **thinks the story or selection** will be about. Thus the teacher is modeling what the students are expected to do later.

Here is an example of a simple second-grade selection:

Find a picture of a bean seed (picture file or encyclopedia)

Title: *From Little Seed to Big Plants*

Predicting: Teacher—"I think that this story is a real or true story. The picture shows a bean seed, and I know that seeds grow into plants. The story might be about how seeds grow into plants. That is my prediction or guess."

Selection: (teacher reads aloud to the students)
"What is in a seed?" asked Betty.
Betty's brother gave her a big bean and said, "Cut this open and see."
Betty cut the bean open. She found a baby plant in the bean.
Betty asked her brother if another bean seed would grow if she planted it.
Betty planted the seed and watered it every day.
When Betty saw the leaves on the plant, she wanted to show them to everyone.

Retelling: Teacher—"The main characters are Betty and her older brother. I think Betty was about seven years old. Her brother might have been in high school. (*Problem*) Betty wanted to know what was in a seed. This led Betty to actually grow the seed. I think Betty's brother helped her learn about seeds and how they grow. (*Outcome*) Betty saw the little plant in the seed. After she grew the seed, she learned that seeds grow into plants. I know that Betty was proud of her plant because she wanted to show everybody her new bean plant."

<u>Note:</u> The teacher never asked the students to predict or retell any part of the title or selection. The teacher did everything possible to **model** the procedure for the students.

The previous procedure is one way to prepare students for Form B: Reader Response Evaluation.

Summary of Specific Instructions—Form B: Reader Response Format

Step 1 The teacher needs to determine if the student understands the story/selection.

Step 2 If the student appears to have the ability to predict and retell the story, do not interrupt with prompting. Strive for a free flow of information.

Step 3 The questions used in the story guide at each grade level are merely suggestions. Feel free to modify or rephrase them.

Step 4 Take notes or use key words when the student is predicting and retelling on the Inventory Record Form.

Step 5 The teacher might like to tape record the student's responses to review the student's retelling at a later time.

Step 6 Once you become proficient in your ability to hear, prompt, and score retellings, you may not always need to use the tape recorder. However, even when you become proficient, you may want to check your skills occasionally by using the tape recorder.

CRI SCORING AND INTERPRETATION

Reader Response Format
Form B: Pretest and Form B: Posttest

The following is a sample CRI record. This example is designed to enable the teacher to gain information on the scoring and interpretation of the Classroom Reading Inventory–Reader Response Format. The sample contains the following:

- A dialog for *getting started* with a student.
- Examples for scoring a student's responses.
- A sample Inventory Record–Reader Response Format for a second grader—Joan.
- A sample Inventory Record–Summary Sheet for Joan, to illustrate how to use and interpret Form B: Reader Response Format.

Getting Started Dialog:

Ms. Sage:	Joan, if I use words like *predict* or *prediction,* do you know what I mean?
Joan:	No.
Ms. Sage:	How about words like *guess* or *making guesses?*
Joan:	Yes, because I know how to guess.
Ms. Sage:	OK, let's practice making a guess. What do you think the cafeteria is having for lunch today?
Joan:	I don't know.
Ms. Sage:	OK, but you said you knew how to guess. How about making a guess? You don't have to be right. All you need to do is make a guess.
Joan:	I think they are having hamburgers.
Ms. Sage:	How will you actually know if they are having hamburgers?
Joan:	When I go to lunch.
Ms. Sage:	Joan, you made a good guess. Let's make more guesses now. I'm going to read you the **title of a story,** and I would like you to make guesses about what the story **might** be about.

Note: Since Joan is a second grader, the second-level selection "Fish for Sale" was selected as a place to start the testing.

Scoring a Student's Responses

The Inventory Record for Teachers directs the teacher to score student responses in the areas of Prediction: Title; Retelling: Character(s), Problem(s), and Outcome(s), on a scale of 1 – 2 – 3. On this scale a score of 1 is low, a score of 2 is average, and a score of 3 is high.

Using Prediction as an example, the teacher would score the student as a 3 (high) if the student was able to predict the story content without any prompting. The teacher would score the student as a 2 (average) if the student was able to predict the story content with only some *general* prompting. The teacher would score the student as a 1 (low) if the student needed *suggestive* and *specific* prompting.

For the areas of Prediction: Title; Retelling: Character(s), Problem(s), and Outcome(s), the total scoring will be as follows:

TOTAL SCORE

10–12	comprehension excellent
6–9	comprehension needs assistance
5 or less	comprehension inadequate

Form B: Pretest Inventory Record
Summary Sheet

Student's Name: _____ *Joan* _____ **Grade:** ___ *2* ___ **Age:** _*7-6*_
year, months

Date: _*Today*_ **School:** _____ *Troost* _____ **Administered by:** ___ *J. White* ___

	Predicting-Retelling					Reading Level		
Level	Prediction	Character(s)	Problem(s)	Outcome(s) Solution(s)	TOTAL	IND	INST	FRUST
1.								
2.	3	3	3	3	12	✓		
3.	3	1	1	1	6			✓
4.								
5.								
6.								
7.								
8.								

Summary of Responses:

Ability to Predict: _____ *Joan understands and is willing to make predictions.* _____

_____

Ability to Retell: _____ *At the 2nd level, she appears to comprehend the selection.*

However, at the 3rd level, she needed help with characters, problems, and outcomes.

Prompting to Obtain Predicting and Retelling Responses: _____ *Considerable prompting was needed*

at the 3rd level.

Reading Level: _*Joan is independent with 2nd-level material.*_

Comments: _____ *Joan needs specific retelling practice. She appears to be a good reader for her*

age and grade level.

Form B: Pretest, Level 2

FISH FOR SALE

Susan got ten fish and a tank for her birthday. She loved the fish and learned to take good care of them.

One day Susan saw six new baby fish in the tank. The fish tank was too small for all of the fish. Dad said he would buy another tank for the baby fish.

Everyone began giving Susan fish and equipment. Soon she had tanks for big fish, small fish, and baby fish.

Each tank had water plants, air tubes, and stones on the bottom.

Mom said, "Enough! Susan, your room looks like a store for fish."

That gave Susan an idea. Why not put all of the fish tanks in the garage and put up a sign? Susan and her dad moved everything into the garage.

Susan made a big sign that read, "FISH FOR SALE."

Student Responses

Low – High (Circle number)
1   2   3

PREDICTION:
Title   1   2   ③
What do you think is meant by the title, "Fish for Sale"? What do you think the story will be about?

A kid wanted to buy a fish.

The fish are on sale.

_____

RETELLING:

Character(s)   1   2   ③
What do you remember about the people in the story?

Susan got a fish for her birthday. The fish
had baby fish—six I think the story said.

_____

Problem(s)   1   2   ③
What was the problem? What would you do if you had this problem?

Too many fish. Susan needed more tanks.
Susan's mother was upset. The room was
messy. I'd keep the room clean.

Outcome(s)/Solution(s) 1   2   ③
How was the problem solved? What do you think Susan's goal was?

Susan and her dad moved the fish tanks to
the garage. Susan got the idea to make a
sign and sell the fish.

SCORING GUIDE

TOTAL SCORE _12_

		Prompting		Reading Level	
(10–12)	Comprehension excellent	None	✓		
6–9	Comprehension needs assistance	General	___	IND	✓
5 or less	Comprehension inadequate	Specific	___	INST	___
		Suggestive	___	FRUST	___

Form B: Pretest, Level 3

SILLY BIRDS

    With food all around them, baby turkeys will not eat. They don't know food when they see it. They often die for lack of water. Water is always kept in their bowls, but some of these birds never seem to discover what the water is for. We have a hard time trying to understand these silly birds.

    Baby turkeys don't know enough to come out of the rain either. So many of the silly young birds catch cold and die. If they see anything bright, they will try to eat it. It may be a coin, a small nail, or even a shovel. You can see how foolish these silly birds are.

Student Responses

Low   –   High   **(Circle number)**
1   2   3

PREDICTION:
Title   1   2   (3)
This story is about turkeys. Why do you think they are called silly birds?

Maybe because they do silly things like try

to run away.

RETELLING:
Character(s)   (1)   2   3
Can you tell me what the story said about turkeys?

That they were silly.

Problem(s)   (1)   2   3
What did the story say about turkeys eating and not eating?

That they would not eat (why not?).

They weren't hungry.

Outcome(s)/Solution(s) (1)   2   3
Can you tell me what happens to turkeys when they do silly things?

They don't get anything to eat.

SCORING GUIDE

TOTAL SCORE   _6_

		Prompting		Reading Level	
10–12	Comprehension excellent	None	____		
(6–9)	Comprehension needs assistance	General	____	IND	____
5 or less	Comprehension inadequate	Specific	✓	INST	____
		Suggestive	✓	FRUST	✓

Summary of Specific Instructions

Step 1   Establish rapport. Don't be in a hurry to begin testing. Put the student at ease. Make him/her feel comfortable.

Step 2   Begin at the level of the student's current grade level. If, for example, the student is a third grader, begin with a third-grade selection. If the student has the ability to predict and retell, and is reading comfortably, go to the fourth-grade-level selection. If the student is having difficulty, drop back to the second-grade-level selection. If you have reason to believe that the student is reading above or below grade level, adjust the starting level accordingly.

Step 3   Read the title aloud. Take care to cover the selection while reading. Using the title, ask the student to predict, to make guesses about the selection. If necessary, use a prompting strategy.

Step 4   Have the student read the selection aloud to you. After reading, ask the student to retell the story by noting character(s), problem(s), and outcome(s)/solution(s). The guided questions listed for the predicting and retelling scorable areas are merely suggestions. Feel free to change them as needed.

Step 5   If it becomes necessary to prompt, use a *general* prompt first so as to not give the story away. If the student needs *suggestive* or *specific* prompting, it is safe to assume that the student is having difficulty comprehending what s/he is reading.

Step 6   As previously stated, the Independent Reading Level is the level at which the student is able to read without difficulty; i.e., the oral reading of the story is fluent and expressive; there are few if any significant word recognition errors. During the retelling, the student has no difficulty in recalling the character(s), the problem(s), and the outcome(s)/solution(s).

Step 7   Transfer the Independent Reading Level and the scorable parts total to the Inventory Record–Summary Sheet.

READER RESPONSE FORMAT
FORM B: PRETEST

Graded Paragraphs

IT'S MY BALL

Tom and Nancy went for a walk.

They saw a small ball on the grass.

They began fighting over the ball.

While they were fighting, a dog picked up the ball and ran.

The kids ran after the dog, but the dog got away.

FISH FOR SALE

Susan got ten fish and a tank for her birthday.

She loved the fish and learned to take good care of them.

One day, Susan saw six new baby fish in the tank.

The fish tank was too small for all of the fish.

Dad said he would buy another tank for the baby fish.

Everyone began giving Susan fish and equipment.

Soon she had tanks for big fish, small fish, and baby fish.

Each tank had water plants, air tubes, and stones on the bottom.

Mom said, "Enough! Susan, your room looks like a store for fish."

That gave Susan an idea. Why not put all of the fish tanks in the garage and put up a sign?

Susan and her dad moved everything into the garage.

Susan made a big sign that read, "FISH FOR SALE."

SILLY BIRDS

With food all around them, baby turkeys will not eat. They don't know food when they see it. They often die for lack of water. Water is always kept in their bowls, but some of these birds never seem to discover what the water is for. We have a hard time trying to understand these silly birds.

Baby turkeys don't know enough to come out of the rain either. So many of the silly young birds catch cold and die. If they see anything bright, they will try to eat it. It may be a coin, a small nail, or even a shovel. You can see how foolish these silly birds are.

ALONG THE OREGON TRAIL

This is a story about one family that traveled along the Oregon Trail. We will call this family the Mortons. Their son, Andrew, wrote this journal with the help of his sister, Emily. Here are some entries from Andrew's journal.

March 31, 1848:	Hurray! Today we leave St. Louis and take a steamboat up the Missouri River to Independence, Missouri. Emily can hardly stop talking.
April 7, 1848:	Today we arrived in Independence. Emily asked Pa how long the trip would take from here. He told her six months.
May 5, 1848:	The wagonmaster told us to keep a sharp lookout for Indians. Emily says she's not afraid.
June 16, 1848:	Tomorrow we reach Fort Laramie. Ma said we've come more than 700 miles.
July 11, 1848:	We are now climbing up the Rocky Mountains. The nights are cold.
July 20, 1848:	We have come down from the mountains. The weather is scorching hot.
August 15, 1848:	Today we reached Fort Hall. The soldiers gave us antelope steaks and turnips for dinner. Emily says she hates turnips.
November 12, 1848:	We are near the Willamette River Valley. We shall soon see the place where we will make our new home. Emily calls this the promised land.

THE FOX—A FARMER'S BEST FRIEND

"Meg, look! That's a female fox ready to have cubs." Uncle Mike was excited, "I haven't seen a fox around here for ten years." Meg said, "Shall I get your gun?" "There's no need for a gun," Uncle Mike replied. "Foxes help farmers by eating pests like mice, squirrels, frogs, and insects."

The next day Meg and her uncle were unhappy to learn that some farmers were hunting for the fox. These farmers didn't believe that a fox was helpful. Foxes save the farmers' crops by eating pests that destroy their crops. The farmers were sure that foxes only killed chickens and other small animals.

After weeks of hunting, the farmers gave up trying to kill the fox. When Uncle Mike and Meg found fresh fox and cub tracks on the far end of their farm, they were pleased the fox had not been killed.

HUSH MY BABY

Nate was a slave who lived with his master in Baltimore. Nate wanted freedom. He got an idea. "What if I build a big box, big enough so I could hide in it?" Nate got busy, and when the box was built, he got inside of it. Nate's uncle put the box on a ship that was going to New York. It was very cold in the box. Nate was afraid he would not make it to freedom.

On a Sunday morning, the ship arrived in New York. Nate's friend John was waiting at the dock. The ship's captain told John they didn't deliver boxes on Sunday. John worried that Nate might die from being in the box too long. He talked the captain into letting him take the box with him.

While the captain was helping John load the box onto a wagon, Nate sneezed. John was afraid that Nate would be discovered and sent back to his owner. To cover the noise of Nate's sneeze, John started singing "Hush My Baby." This also warned Nate to be very quiet. At last the box was delivered to the right house. It was opened, and out popped Nate, cold and stiff—but happy and free!

THE GOLDEN DOOR

The year was 1892. A ship crowded with people from many parts of the world was nearing New York City.

Jacob Goldberg stood at the ship's rail waiting. Jacob and his family were forced to leave their home in Russia because of the violent anti-Jewish attacks that took place there.

Beside Jacob at the ship's rail stood Nunzio Genetti. Nunzio and Jacob had become friends during the long sea voyage, even though neither one could speak the other's language. Nunzio and his family had to leave their small village in Italy because there was no work for the people.

As the ship came into New York Harbor, the boys' eyes widened. There, in the middle of the harbor, stood the *Lady with the Lamp*—the Statue of Liberty.

Many people crowded the rail beside Jacob and Nunzio. They began crying and cheering at the same time.

Surely, here was the *Golden Door* through which to pass to a better life.

THE WORLD OF DINOSAURS

Before the 1800s, no one knew that dinosaurs had ever existed. Once in a while, people would find a dinosaur tooth or bone but did not realize what it was.

When dinosaurs lived, the earth was not like it is today. Mountains like the Alps, for example, had not yet been formed.

The first dinosaur appeared on the earth about 220 million years ago. For 150 million years or so, they ruled the earth. Suddenly, about 63 million years ago, dinosaurs died out.

What caused this "terrible lizard," for that is what *dinosaur* means in English, to die out so suddenly?

Scientists have developed lots of theories to try to explain what happened to the dinosaurs. One theory is that the earth became too cold for them.

Most scientists believe that no single theory explains what happened to the dinosaurs. It may be that they could not keep up with the way the earth was changing. Whatever the cause, or causes, it was the end of the World of Dinosaurs.

READER RESPONSE FORMAT
FORM B: PRETEST

Inventory Record for Teachers

Form B: Pretest Inventory Record
Summary Sheet

Student's Name: _____ **Grade:** _____ **Age:** _____

year, months

Date: _____ **School:** _____ **Administered by:** _____

	Predicting-Retelling					Reading Level		
Level	Prediction	Character(s)	Problem(s)	Outcome(s) Solution(s)	TOTAL	IND	INST	FRUST
1.								
2.								
3.								
4.								
5.								
6.								
7.								
8.								

Summary of Responses:

Ability to Predict: _____

_____

_____

Ability to Retell: _____

_____

_____

Prompting to Obtain Predicting and Retelling Responses: _____

_____

_____

Reading Level: _____

Comments: _____

_____

Form B: Pretest, Level 1

IT'S MY BALL

Tom and Nancy went for a walk.

They saw a small ball on the grass.

They began fighting over the ball.

While they were fighting, a dog picked up the ball

and ran.

The kids ran after the dog, but the dog got away.

Student Responses

Low – High   (Circle number)
1   2   3

PREDICTION:
Title   1   2   3
What do you think the story will be about?

_____

_____

_____

RETELLING:

Character(s)   1   2   3
What do you remember about the people in the story?

_____

_____

_____

Problem(s)   1   2   3
What was the problem? If you were in that situation, what would you do?

_____

_____

_____

Outcome(s)/Solution(s) 1   2   3
How was the problem solved?

_____

_____

_____

SCORING GUIDE

TOTAL SCORE _____		Prompting		Reading Level	
10–12	Comprehension excellent	None	_____		
6–9	Comprehension needs assistance	General	_____	IND	_____
5 or less	Comprehension inadequate	Specific	_____	INST	_____
		Suggestive	_____	FRUST	_____

Form B: Pretest, Level 2

FISH FOR SALE

Susan got ten fish and a tank for her birthday. She loved the fish and learned to take good care of them.

One day, Susan saw six new baby fish in the tank. The fish tank was too small for all of the fish. Dad said he would buy another tank for the baby fish.

Everyone began giving Susan fish and equipment. Soon she had tanks for big fish, small fish, and baby fish.

Each tank had water plants, air tubes, and stones on the bottom.

Mom said, "Enough! Susan, your room looks like a store for fish."

That gave Susan an idea. Why not put all of the fish tanks in the garage and put up a sign?

Susan and her dad moved everything into the garage.

Susan made a big sign that read, "FISH FOR SALE."

Student Responses

Low – High   (Circle number)
1   2   3

PREDICTION:
Title   1   2   3
What do you think is meant by the title "Fish for Sale"? What do you think the story will be about?

_____
_____
_____

RETELLING:
Character(s)   1   2   3
What do you remember about the people in the story?

_____
_____
_____

Problem(s)   1   2   3
What was the problem? What would you do if you had this problem?

_____
_____
_____

Outcome(s)/Solution(s) 1   2   3
How was the problem solved? What do you think Susan's goal was?

_____
_____
_____

SCORING GUIDE

TOTAL SCORE _____

		Prompting		Reading Level	
10–12	Comprehension excellent	None	_____		
6–9	Comprehension needs assistance	General	_____	IND	_____
5 or less	Comprehension inadequate	Specific	_____	INST	_____
		Suggestive	_____	FRUST	_____

Form B: Pretest, Level 3

SILLY BIRDS

With food all around them, baby turkeys will not eat. They don't know food when they see it. They often die for lack of water. Water is always kept in their bowls, but some of these birds never seem to discover what the water is for. We have a hard time trying to understand these silly birds.

Baby turkeys don't know enough to come out of the rain either. So many of the silly young birds catch cold and die. If they see anything bright, they will try to eat it. It may be a coin, a small nail, or even a shovel. You can see how foolish these silly birds are.

Student Responses

Low   –   High   (Circle number)
1   2   3

PREDICTION:
Title   1   2   3
This story is about turkeys. Why do you think they are called silly birds?

_____

_____

_____

RETELLING:
Character(s)   1   2   3
Can you tell me what the story said about turkeys?

_____

_____

_____

Problem(s)   1   2   3
What did the story say about turkeys eating and not eating?

_____

_____

_____

Outcome(s)/Solution(s) 1   2   3
Can you tell me what happens to turkeys when they do silly things?

_____

_____

_____

SCORING GUIDE

TOTAL SCORE _____		Prompting		Reading Level	
10–12	Comprehension excellent	None	_____		
6–9	Comprehension needs assistance	General	_____	IND	_____
5 or less	Comprehension inadequate	Specific	_____	INST	_____
		Suggestive	_____	FRUST	_____

Form B: Pretest, Level 4

ALONG THE OREGON TRAIL

This is a story about one family that traveled along the Oregon Trail. We will call this family the Mortons. Their son, Andrew, wrote this journal with the help of his sister, Emily. Here are some entries from Andrew's journal.

March 31, 1848:
 Hurray! Today we leave St. Louis and take a steamboat up the Missouri River to Independence, Missouri. Emily can hardly stop talking.

April 7, 1848:
 Today we arrived in Independence. Emily asked Pa how long the trip would take from here. He told her six months.

May 5, 1848:
 The wagonmaster told us to keep a sharp lookout for Indians. Emily says she's not afraid.

June 16, 1848:
 Tomorrow we reach Fort Laramie. Ma said we've come more than 700 miles.

July 11, 1848:
 We are now climbing up the Rocky Mountains. The nights are cold.

July 20, 1848:
 We have come down from the mountains. The weather is scorching hot.

August 15, 1848:
 Today we reached Fort Hall. The soldiers gave us antelope steaks and turnips for dinner. Emily says she hates turnips.

November 12, 1848:
 We are near the Willamette River Valley. We shall soon see the place where we will make our new home. Emily calls this the promised land.

Student Responses

Low – High   (Circle number)
1   2   3

PREDICTION:
Title   1   2   3
What can you tell me about pioneers? What do you think pioneers have to do with the Oregon Trail?

_____

_____

_____

RETELLING:
Character(s)   1   2   3
What can you tell me about Andrew and Emily?

_____

_____

_____

Problem(s)   1   2   3
What were some of the hardships they faced?

_____

_____

_____

Outcome(s)/Solution(s) 1   2   3
What happened to Andrew and Emily?

_____

_____

_____

SCORING GUIDE

TOTAL SCORE _____		Prompting		Reading Level	
10–12	Comprehension excellent	None	_____		
6–9	Comprehension needs assistance	General	_____	IND	_____
5 or less	Comprehension inadequate	Specific	_____	INST	_____
		Suggestive	_____	FRUST	_____

THE FOX—A FARMER'S BEST FRIEND

"Meg, look! That's a female fox ready to have cubs." Uncle Mike was excited, "I haven't seen a fox around here for ten years." Meg said, "Shall I get your gun?" "There's no need for a gun," Uncle Mike replied. "Foxes help farmers by eating pests like mice, squirrels, frogs, and insects."

The next day Meg and her uncle were unhappy to learn that some farmers were hunting for the fox. These farmers didn't believe that a fox was helpful. Foxes save the farmers' crops by eating pests that destroy their crops. The farmers were sure that foxes only killed chickens and other small animals.

After weeks of hunting, the farmers gave up trying to kill the fox. When Uncle Mike and Meg found fresh fox and cub tracks on the far end of their farm, they were pleased the fox had not been killed.

Student Responses

Low – High   (Circle number)
1   2   3

PREDICTION:
Title   1   2   3
Have you ever seen a fox? If not, discuss things about a fox. What do you think the story will be about?

_____

_____

_____

RETELLING:
Character(s)   1   2   3
What can you tell me about the people in the story?

_____

_____

_____

Problem(s)   1   2   3
The fox had a problem. What do you think was happening? Why do you think Meg and Uncle Mike worried?

_____

_____

Outcome(s)/Solution(s) 1   2   3
What happened to the fox? When Uncle Mike and Meg saw the tracks, what did they learn? How did Uncle Mike and Meg feel?

_____

_____

_____

SCORING GUIDE

TOTAL SCORE _____

		Prompting		Reading Level	
10–12	Comprehension excellent	None	_____		
6–9	Comprehension needs assistance	General	_____	IND	_____
5 or less	Comprehension inadequate	Specific	_____	INST	_____
		Suggestive	_____	FRUST	_____

Form B: Pretest, Level 6

HUSH MY BABY

Nate was a slave who lived with his master in Baltimore. Nate wanted freedom. He got an idea. "What if I build a big box, big enough so I could hide in it?" Nate got busy, and when the box was built, he got inside of it. Nate's uncle put the box on a ship that was going to New York. It was very cold in the box. Nate was afraid he would not make it to freedom.

On a Sunday morning, the ship arrived in New York. Nate's friend John was waiting at the dock. The ship's captain told John they didn't deliver boxes on Sunday. John worried that Nate might die from being in the box too long. He talked the captain into letting him take the box with him.

While the captain was helping John load the box onto a wagon, Nate sneezed. John was afraid that Nate would be discovered and sent back to his owner. To cover the noise of Nate's sneeze, John started singing "Hush My Baby". This also warned Nate to be very quiet. At last the box was delivered to the right house. It was opened, and out popped Nate, cold and stiff—but happy and free!

Student Responses

Low   –   High   (Circle number)
1   2   3

PREDICTION:
Title   1   2   3
This is a story about a slave. What can you tell me about slaves?

_____

_____

RETELLING:
Character(s)   1   2   3
Who was Nate and what did he want to do?

_____

_____

Problem(s)   1   2   3
What problem did Nate try to solve?

_____

_____

Outcome(s)/Solution(s) 1   2   3
What happened to Nate?

_____

_____

_____

SCORING GUIDE

TOTAL SCORE _____		Prompting		Reading Level	
10–12	Comprehension excellent	None	_____		
6–9	Comprehension needs assistance	General	_____	IND	_____
5 or less	Comprehension inadequate	Specific	_____	INST	_____
		Suggestive	_____	FRUST	_____

Form B: Pretest, Level 7

THE GOLDEN DOOR

The year was 1892. A ship crowded with people from many parts of the world was nearing New York City.

Jacob Goldberg stood at the ship's rail waiting. Jacob and his family were forced to leave their home in Russia because of the violent anti-Jewish attacks that took place there.

Beside Jacob at the ship's rail stood Nunzio Genetti. Nunzio and Jacob had become friends during the long sea voyage, even though neither one could speak the other's language. Nunzio and his family had to leave their small village in Italy because there was no work for the people.

As the ship came into New York Harbor, the boys' eyes widened. There, in the middle of the harbor, stood the *Lady with the Lamp*—the Statue of Liberty.

Many people crowded the rail beside Jacob and Nunzio. They began crying and cheering at the same time.

Surely, here was the *Golden Door* through which to pass to a better life.

Student Responses

Low – High   (Circle number)
1   2   3

PREDICTION:
Title   1   2   3
What do you think the Statue of Liberty has to do with a Golden Door?

_____

_____

RETELLING:
Character(s)   1   2   3
What can you tell me about the two boys in this story?

_____

_____

Problem(s)   1   2   3
Why did these families leave their homes?

_____

_____

Outcome(s)/Solution(s) 1   2   3
What did they hope to find in America?

_____

_____

_____

SCORING GUIDE

TOTAL SCORE _____		Prompting		Reading Level	
10–12	Comprehension excellent	None	_____		
6–9	Comprehension needs assistance	General	_____	IND	_____
5 or less	Comprehension inadequate	Specific	_____	INST	_____
		Suggestive	_____	FRUST	_____

Form B: Pretest, Level 8

THE WORLD OF DINOSAURS

Before the 1800s, no one knew that dinosaurs had ever existed. Once in a while, people would find a dinosaur tooth or bone but did not realize what it was.

When dinosaurs lived, the earth was not like it is today. Mountains like the Alps, for example, had not yet been formed.

The first dinosaur appeared on the earth about 220 million years ago. For 150 million years or so, they ruled the earth. Suddenly, about 63 million years ago, dinosaurs died out.

What caused this "terrible lizard," for that is what *dinosaur* means in English, to die out so suddenly?

Scientists have developed lots of theories to try to explain what happened to the dinosaurs. One theory is that the earth became too cold for them.

Most scientists believe that no single theory explains what happened to the dinosaurs. It may be that they could not keep up with the way the earth was changing. Whatever the cause, or causes, it was the end of the World of Dinosaurs.

Student Responses

Low – High   (Circle number)
1   2   3

PREDICTION:
Title   1   2   3
What can you tell me about dinosaurs?

_____

_____

_____

RETELLING:
Character(s)   1   2   3
Tell me what you can about dinosaurs.

_____

_____

_____

Problem(s)   1   2   3
What problem did the dinosaurs have with their environment?

_____

_____

_____

Outcome(s)/Solution(s) 1   2   3
What happened to the dinosaurs?

_____

_____

_____

SCORING GUIDE

TOTAL SCORE _____		Prompting		Reading Level	
10–12	Comprehension excellent	None	_____		
6–9	Comprehension needs assistance	General	_____	IND	_____
5 or less	Comprehension inadequate	Specific	_____	INST	_____
		Suggestive	_____	FRUST	_____

READER RESPONSE FORMAT
FORM B: POSTTEST

Graded Paragraphs

THE RED ANT

The red ant lives under the sand.

The ant must build its own room.

It has to take the sand outside.

The sand is made into little hills.

Building a room is hard work.

The red ant is a busy bug.

WHY CAN'T I PLAY?

Kim wanted to play on the boys' team.

The boys said, "No."

One day the boys needed one more player.

They asked Kim to play.

Kim got the ball and kicked it a long way.

She was a fast runner and a good player.

Todd, a boy on the team, kicked the ball to her.

Kim kicked the ball down the side of the field.

Tony, a boy on the other team, tried to block her.

He missed, and Kim scored.

Someone said, "Kim should have played on the team all year."

FLOODS ARE DANGEROUS

Mrs. Sanchez was driving home with her two sons, Luis and Ernesto. From the darkening sky, Mrs. Sanchez could see that a storm was coming. Soon, lightning flashed, thunder boomed, and the rain poured down. In order to get to her house, Mrs. Sanchez had to cross a road covered with water. She decided to drive across the rushing water. When they were just about across the road, the rising water caused the car to float away. Mrs. Sanchez knew that she had to get the boys and herself out of that car.

Luis was able to roll down the window and jump to dry ground. Mrs. Sanchez also jumped to some dry ground. Mrs. Sanchez and Luis tried to grab Ernesto, but the car floated out of reach.

Soon the police and some friends came, and they searched all night for Ernesto and the car. They were unable to find them. Had Ernesto drowned in the flood, or was he safe?

Early the next day, Mrs. Sanchez saw a police car drive up to her house. Her heart raced when she saw Ernesto in the police car. He was safe! Ernesto told his mother that their car got stuck against a tree and that he was able to climb out of the car. He sat in the tree until daylight when the police saw him. Everyone was happy to see Ernesto again.

FIRST TO DIE

It was very cold that March day in Boston. The year was 1770. It was a time of protest and riots. The people of Boston had had it with British rule.

Nobody knew that the day would end in bloodshed. This was the day of the Boston Massacre—March 5, 1770.

Somewhere in the city that night, a black man and former slave named Crispus Attucks was moving toward his place in history.

The British had brought troops into Boston in 1768. There were fights between the people of Boston and the soldiers.

On the night of March 6, 1770, the streets were filled with men. They were angry. Crispus Attucks was the leader of a patriot crowd of men. They met up with a group of British soldiers. The crowd pushed in on the soldiers. There was much confusion. A soldier fired his rifle. Attucks fell into the gutter—dead.

Crispus Attucks had been a leader in the night's actions. A black man and a former slave, he had helped to bring about action that led to the foundation of American independence.

TIGER

Tiger is hungry. He has not eaten for five days. His last meal was a wild pig. It is dark now, and Tiger is on a hunt. As he slinks through the jungle, the muscles of his powerful neck and shoulders are tense. Tiger senses that there are humans close by. Tiger is careful to avoid humans. He knows that only old or sick tigers will hunt humans because they are no longer swift enough to hunt other animals.

Suddenly, Tiger's sensitive nostrils pick up the scent of an animal. Tiger creeps slowly toward the smell. There, in a clearing in the jungle, he sees a goat. The goat has picked up Tiger's scent. Tiger moves in, but the goat does not flee. It is a trap! Humans have tied the goat there to trap Tiger. Tiger stops, then moves back into the jungle.

Tiger is hungry.

SENTINELS IN THE FOREST

Many wild creatures that travel with their own kind know by instinct how to protect the group. One of them acts as a sentinel.

Hidden by the branches of a low-hanging tree, I once watched two white-tailed deer feeding in a meadow. At first, my interest was held by their beauty. But soon I noticed something strange; they were taking turns feeding. While one was calmly cropping grass, unafraid and at ease, the other—with head high, eyes sweeping the sea marsh, and sensitive nostrils "feeling" the air—stood on guard against enemies. Not for a moment, during the half hour I spied upon them, did they stop their teamwork.

I LOVE A MYSTERY

Ever since the year 1841, when Edgar Allan Poe wrote *The Murders in the Rue Morgue,* people around the world quickly become fans of the mystery/detective story.

The mystery begins with a strange crime. There are a number of clues. A detective is called in to solve the mysterious crime. The clues may lead the detective to or away from the solution. In the end the detective reveals the criminal and tells how the mystery was solved.

The detective in most mystery stories is usually not a regular police officer but a private detective. Probably the most famous of all these private detectives is Sherlock Holmes. With his friend and assistant Dr. Watson, Sherlock Holmes solved many strange crimes.

One of the most popular of all the mysteries that Holmes solved is called *The Hound of the Baskervilles.* In this story a man is murdered, and the only clue Holmes has to go on is an enormous hound's footprints found next to the dead man's body.

Do you love a mystery?

IT CANNOT BE HELPED

There is a phrase the Japanese use when something difficult must be endured—*it cannot be helped.*

On a quiet Sunday morning in early December 1941, the Japanese launched a surprise attack on Pearl Harbor. Shortly after that, the Army and the FBI began rounding up all Japanese who were living along the West Coast of the United States. Every Japanese man, woman, and child, 110,000 of them, was sent to inland prison camps. Even though the Japanese had been living in the United States since 1869, they were never allowed to become citizens. Suddenly, they were a people with no rights who looked exactly like the enemy.

With the closing of the prison camps in the fall of 1945, the families were sent back to the West Coast.

The Japanese relocation program, carried through at such great cost in misery and tragedy, was justified on the ground that the Japanese were potentially disloyal. The record does not show a single case of Japanese disloyalty or sabotage during the whole war.

In June 1952, Congress passed Public Law 414, granting Japanese the right to become United States citizens.

READER RESPONSE FORMAT
FORM B: POSTTEST

Inventory Record for Teachers

Form B: Posttest Inventory Record
Summary Sheet

Student's Name: _____ Grade: _____ Age: _____

year, months

Date: _____ School: _____ Administered by: _____

Level	Predicting-Retelling					Reading Level		
	Prediction	Character(s)	Problem(s)	Outcome(s) Solution(s)	TOTAL	IND	INST	FRUST
1.								
2.								
3.								
4.								
5.								
6.								
7.								
8.								

Summary of Responses:

Ability to Predict: _____

_____

_____

Ability to Retell: _____

_____

_____

Prompting to Obtain Predicting and Retelling Responses: _____

_____

_____

Reading Level: _____

Comments: _____

_____

Form B: Posttest, Level 1

THE RED ANT

The red ant lives under the sand.

The ant must build its own room.

It has to take the sand outside.

The sand is made into little hills.

Building a room is hard work.

The red ant is a busy bug.

Student Responses

Low – High   (Circle number)
1   2   3

PREDICTION:
Title   1   2   3
What do you think the story will be about?

_____

_____

_____

RETELLING:
Character(s)   1   2   3
What can you tell me about the red ant?

_____

_____

_____

Problem(s)   1   2   3
What did the red ant have to do to build its room?

_____

_____

_____

Outcome(s)/Solution(s) 1   2   3
What can you tell me about the red ant's work habits?

_____

_____

_____

SCORING GUIDE

TOTAL SCORE _____		Prompting		Reading Level	
10–12	Comprehension excellent	None	_____		
6–9	Comprehension needs assistance	General	_____	IND	_____
5 or less	Comprehension inadequate	Specific	_____	INST	_____
		Suggestive	_____	FRUST	_____

Form B: Posttest, Level 2

WHY CAN'T I PLAY?

Kim wanted to play on the boys' team.

The boys said, "No."

One day, the boys needed one more player.

They asked Kim to play.

Kim got the ball and kicked it a long way.

She was a fast runner and a good player.

Todd, a boy on the team, kicked the ball to her.

Kim kicked the ball down the side of the field.

Tony, a boy on the other team, tried to block her.

He missed, and Kim scored.

Someone said, "Kim should have played on the team all year."

Student Responses

Low   –   High   (Circle number)
1   2   3

PREDICTION:
Title   1   2   3
What do you think is meant by the title "Why Can't I Play?" What do you think the story will be about?

_____

_____

_____

RETELLING:
Character(s)   1   2   3
Who was the main person in the story? Can you tell me more about that person?

_____

_____

_____

Problem(s)   1   2   3
What was the problem? Can you tell me anything more?

_____

_____

_____

Outcome(s)/Solution(s) 1   2   3
How was the problem solved?

_____

_____

_____

SCORING GUIDE

TOTAL SCORE _____		Prompting		Reading Level	
10–12	Comprehension excellent	none	_____		
6–9	Comprehension needs assistance	general	_____	IND	_____
5 or less	Comprehension inadequate	specific	_____	INST	_____
		suggestive	_____	FRUST	_____

Form B: Posttest, Level 3

FLOODS ARE DANGEROUS

Mrs. Sanchez was driving home with her two sons, Luis and Ernesto. From the darkening sky, Mrs. Sanchez could see that a storm was coming. Soon, lightning flashed, thunder boomed, and the rain poured down. In order to get to her house, Mrs. Sanchez had to cross a road covered with water. She decided to drive across the rushing water. When they were just about across the road, the rising water caused the car to float away. Mrs. Sanchez knew that she had to get the boys and herself out of that car.

Luis was able to roll down the window and jump to dry ground. Mrs. Sanchez also jumped to some dry ground. Mrs. Sanchez and Luis tried to grab Ernesto, but the car floated out of reach.

Soon the police and some friends came, and they searched all night for Ernesto and the car. They were unable to find them. Had Ernesto drowned in the flood, or was he safe?

Early the next day, Mrs. Sanchez saw a police car drive up to her house. Her heart raced when she saw Ernesto in the police car. He was safe! Ernesto told his mother that their car got stuck against a tree and that he was able to climb out of the car. He sat in the tree until daylight when the police saw him. Everyone was happy to see Ernesto again.

Student Responses

Low   –   High   (Circle number)
1   2   3

PREDICTION:
Title   1   2   3
What do you think can happen if a car tries to cross a road that is flooded?

_____

_____

_____

RETELLING:
Character(s)   1   2   3
What do you remember about the people in the story? How do you think they felt?

_____

_____

_____

Problem(s)   1   2   3
What was the problem? What do you think caused the problem?

_____

_____

_____

Outcome(s)/Solution(s)   1   2   3
How do you think the problem was solved? How do you think you would feel in this situation?

_____

_____

_____

SCORING GUIDE

TOTAL SCORE _____		Prompting		Reading Level	
10–12	Comprehension excellent	None	_____		
6–9	Comprehension needs assistance	General	_____	IND	_____
5 or less	Comprehension inadequate	Specific	_____	INST	_____
		Suggestive	_____	FRUST	_____

Form B: Posttest, Level 4

FIRST TO DIE

It was very cold that March day in Boston. The year was 1770. It was a time of protest and riots. The people of Boston had had it with British rule.

Nobody knew that the day would end in bloodshed. This was the day of the Boston Massacre—March 5, 1770.

Somewhere in the city that night, a black man and former slave named Crispus Attucks was moving toward his place in history.

The British had brought troops into Boston in 1768. There were fights between the people of Boston and the soldiers.

On the night of March 6, 1770, the streets were filled with men. They were angry. Crispus Attucks was the leader of a patriot crowd of men. They met up with a group of British soldiers. The crowd pushed in on the soldiers. There was much confusion. A soldier fired his rifle. Attucks fell into the gutter—dead.

Crispus Attucks had been a leader in the night's actions. A black man and a former slave, he had helped to bring about action that led to the foundation of American independence.

Student Responses

Low – High   (Circle number)
1   2   3

PREDICTION:
Title   1   2   3
This story is about a man named Crispus Attucks. What do you think happened to him?

_____

_____

_____

RETELLING:
Character(s)   1   2   3
What can you tell me about Crispus Attucks?

_____

_____

_____

Problem(s)   1   2   3
What was the problem between the British soldiers and the people of Boston?

_____

_____

_____

Outcome(s)/Solution(s) 1   2   3
What happened to Attucks? What was the result of what he did?

_____

_____

_____

SCORING GUIDE

TOTAL SCORE _____		Prompting		Reading Level	
10–12	Comprehension excellent	None	_____		
6–9	Comprehension needs assistance	General	_____	IND	_____
5 or less	Comprehension inadequate	Specific	_____	INST	_____
		Suggestive	_____	FRUST	_____

Form B: Posttest, Level 5

TIGER

Tiger is hungry. He has not eaten for five days. His last meal was a wild pig. It is dark now, and Tiger is on a hunt. As he slinks through the jungle, the muscles of his powerful neck and shoulders are tense. Tiger senses that there are humans close by. Tiger is careful to avoid humans. He knows that only old or sick tigers will hunt humans because they are no longer swift enough to hunt other animals.

Suddenly, Tiger's sensitive nostrils pick up the scent of an animal. Tiger creeps slowly toward the smell. There, in a clearing in the jungle, he sees a goat. The goat has picked up Tiger's scent. Tiger moves in, but the goat does not flee. It is a trap! Humans have tied the goat there to trap Tiger. Tiger stops, then moves back into the jungle.

Tiger is hungry.

Student Responses

Low – High   (Circle number)
1   2   3

PREDICTION:
Title   1   2   3
Have you ever seen a tiger? What can you tell me about tigers?

_____

_____

_____

RETELLING:
Character(s)   1   2   3
Tell me what happened to Tiger in this story.

_____

_____

_____

Problem(s)   1   2   3
Tiger had a problem. What was it? What did he do?

_____

_____

_____

Outcome(s)/Solution(s) 1   2   3
What happened to Tiger? Why wasn't Tiger trapped?

_____

_____

_____

SCORING GUIDE

TOTAL SCORE _____		Prompting		Reading Level	
10–12	Comprehension excellent	None	_____		
6–9	Comprehension needs assistance	General	_____	IND	_____
5 or less	Comprehension inadequate	Specific	_____	INST	_____
		Suggestive	_____	FRUST	_____

Form B: Posttest, Level 6

SENTINELS IN THE FOREST

Many wild creatures that travel with their own kind know by instinct how to protect the group. One of them acts as a sentinel.

Hidden by the branches of a low-hanging tree, I once watched two white-tailed deer feeding in a meadow. At first, my interest was held by their beauty. But soon I noticed something strange; they were taking turns feeding. While one was calmly cropping grass, unafraid and at ease, the other—with head high, eyes sweeping the sea marsh, and sensitive nostrils "feeling" the air— stood on guard against enemies. Not for a moment, during the half hour I spied upon them, did they stop their teamwork.

Student Responses

Low – High (Circle number)
1 2 3

PREDICTION:
Title 1 2 3
What will this story be about?

_____

_____

_____

RETELLING:
Character(s) 1 2 3
This story is not about a person. Can you tell about the animals in the story?

_____

_____

_____

Problem(s) 1 2 3
Tell about what the animals were doing.

_____

_____

_____

Outcome(s)/Solution(s) 1 2 3
Do you think the animals were good at what they were doing? Tell me more about it.

_____

_____

_____

SCORING GUIDE

TOTAL SCORE _____		Prompting		Reading Level	
10–12	Comprehension excellent	None	_____		
6–9	Comprehension needs assistance	General	_____	IND	_____
5 or less	Comprehension inadequate	Specific	_____	INST	_____
		Suggestive	_____	FRUST	_____

Form B: Posttest, Level 7

I LOVE A MYSTERY

Ever since the year 1841, when Edgar Allan Poe wrote *The Murders in the Rue Morgue*, people around the world quickly become fans of the mystery/detective story.

The mystery begins with a strange crime. There are a number of clues. A detective is called in to solve the mysterious crime. The clues may lead the detective to or away from the solution. In the end the detective reveals the criminal and tells how the mystery was solved.

The detective in most mystery stories is usually not a regular police officer but a private detective. Probably the most famous of all these private detectives is Sherlock Holmes. With his friend and assistant Dr. Watson, Sherlock Holmes solved many strange crimes.

One of the most popular of all the mysteries that Holmes solved is called *The Hound of the Baskervilles*. In this story a man is murdered, and the only clue Holmes has to go on is an enormous hound's footprints found next to the dead man's body.

Do you love a mystery?

Student Responses

Low   –   High   (Circle number)
1   2   3

PREDICTION:
Title   1   2   3
Tell me why you think this story is called "I Love a Mystery."

_____

_____

RETELLING:
Character(s)   1   2   3
What kind of a person is this story about?

_____

_____

Problem(s)   1   2   3
What problems do these people have?

_____

_____

Outcome(s)/Solution(s) 1   2   3
How do they do what they do?

_____

_____

_____

SCORING GUIDE

TOTAL SCORE _____		Prompting		Reading Level	
10–12	Comprehension excellent	None	_____		
6–9	Comprehension needs assistance	General	_____	IND	_____
5 or less	Comprehension inadequate	Specific	_____	INST	_____
		Suggestive	_____	FRUST	_____

Form B: Posttest, Level 8

IT CANNOT BE HELPED

There is a phrase the Japanese use when something difficult must be endured—*it cannot be helped*.

On a quiet Sunday morning in early December of 1941, the Japanese launched a surprise attack on Pearl Harbor. Shortly after that, the Army and the FBI began rounding up all Japanese who were living along the West Coast of the United States. Every Japanese man, woman, and child, 110,000 of them, was sent to inland prison camps. Even though the Japanese had been living in the United States since 1869, they were never allowed to become citizens. Suddenly, they were a people with no rights who looked exactly like the enemy.

With the closing of the prison camps in the fall of 1945, the families were sent back to the West Coast.

The Japanese relocation program, carried through at such great cost in misery and tragedy, was justified on the ground that the Japanese were potentially disloyal. The record does not show a single case of Japanese disloyalty or sabotage during the whole war.

In June 1952, Congress passed Public Law 414, granting Japanese the right to become United States citizens.

Student Responses

Low   –   High   (Circle number)
1   2   3

PREDICTION:
Title   1   2   3
What do you think is meant by this title?

_____

_____

_____

RETELLING:
Character(s)   1   2   3
What happened to the people in this story?

_____

_____

_____

Problem(s)   1   2   3
Why were these people treated this way?

_____

_____

_____

Outcome(s)/Solution(s) 1   2   3
What happened after the war?

_____

_____

_____

SCORING GUIDE

TOTAL SCORE _____		Prompting		Reading Level	
10–12	Comprehension excellent	None	_____		
6–9	Comprehension needs assistance	General	_____	IND	_____
5 or less	Comprehension inadequate	Specific	_____	INST	_____
		Suggestive	_____	FRUST	_____

GLOSSARY OF KEY TERMS

- **Comprehension:** The process of constructing meaning from print.
- **Context Reader:** A student whose decoding skills are inadequate but who can usually answer questions based on the words decoded and background knowledge of the material.
- **Decoding:** Using a variety of skills, including phonics, to determine the spoken equivalent of a printed word.
- **Frustration Level:** The level at which adequate functioning in reading breaks down. Word recognition accuracy drops to 90 percent or lower. Comprehension is at 50 percent or lower. Only one of the two conditions needs to be met for a student to be at the frustration level—word recognition and/or comprehension.
- **Informal Reading Inventory:** A set of graded word lists and passages used to estimate students' oral and silent reading skills.
- **Independent Level:** Adequate functioning in reading with no help from the teacher. Adequate functioning means 99 percent accuracy in word recognition and 90 percent comprehension or better.
- **Instructional Level:** Adequate functioning in reading with help from the teacher. Adequate functioning means 95 percent accuracy in word recognition and 75 percent comprehension or better.
- **Listening Capacity Level:** Adequate understanding of the material that is read to the student by the examiner. A score of 70 percent or better is an indication of adequate understanding.
- **Miscue:** An oral reading response that is different from the correct response. It assumes that the reader is trying to make sense of what is being read. Miscues are not random errors.
- **Norm-Referenced Tests:** Tests that compare students with a representative sample of others who are the same age or in the same grade. The scores indicate whether students did as well as the average, better than the average, or below the average. These tests are not a very good source of information for assessing or planning classroom instruction.
- **Phonics:** Ways of teaching children sound-symbol relationships to help them sound out words.
- **Predictions:** Guesses or inferences made on the basis of prior knowledge.
- **Readability:** An estimate of the difficulty level of text.
- **Reader Response Format:** A format that follows the type of literacy program that challenges students to use their inferential and critical reading and thinking abilities.
- **Reading Levels:** See Independent Level, Instructional Level, Frustration Level, and Listening Capacity Level.
- **Structural Analysis:** Ways of teaching children how to break up longer words into pronounceable units.
- **Subskills Format:** Format that enables the teacher to diagnose a student's ability to decode words both in isolation and context and to answer questions.
- **Word Caller:** A student who is quite proficient at decoding words but does not assign meaning to the words decoded.
- **Word Recognition:** The ability to determine the oral equivalent of a printed word. It does not involve determining word meaning. The reader can recognize the word without knowing its meaning.

GLOSSARY OF BASIC
DECODING TERMINOLOGY

- **Consonants:**   All the letters of the alphabet except the vowels.
- **Consonant Blends:**   Two- and three- letter consonant clusters in which each consonant letter retains some of its regular consonant sound; e.g., say the word *blend;* you should be able to hear both the *b* sound and the *l* sound.
- **Consonant Digraphs:**   Sound made when two consonant letters are joined together. For example, the consonant *t* has its own sound as in *top* and *h* has its own sound as in *help.* However, when *t* and *h* are joined in a word such as *them,* a new sound—a consonant digraph—is produced. *Th, wh, ch, ng,* and *sh* are five of the most common consonant digraphs.
- **Fluency:**   Reading in an expressive manner without any significant word recognition difficulty.
- **Grapheme:**   A letter or letters that represent a speech sound.
- **Phoneme:**   A sound in a language.
- **Phoneme-Grapheme Correspondence:**   The association between a sound (phoneme) and the letter (grapheme) that represents it.
- **Prefix:**   A beginning syllable that modifies the meaning of a word usually called a root word; e.g., *re* (again), the prefix, plus *start,* the root word = *restart,* to start again. See also Root Word and Suffix.
- **Rime:**   A vowel and any following consonant of a syllable; e.g., *at* as in *cat, ike* as in *bike.*
- **Root Word:**   A word of usually one or two syllables to which prefixes and suffixes are added; e.g., the root word *play* + the prefix *re* + the suffix *ed* = *replayed.*
- **Sight Word:**   A word that is recognized instantly and automatically on sight as a whole word and without phonetic analysis; e.g., *the, and.*
- **Suffix:**   Letters added after a root word to change the meaning of the word; e.g., the suffixer + the root word *read* = the noun *reader.*
- **Syllable:**   A group of letters containing only one vowel sound; e.g., *paper* is a two-syllable word— *pa / per.* Only one vowel per syllable.
- **Vowels:**   Sounds represented by the letters, *a, e, i, o, u,* and sometimes *y* and *w.*
- **Vowel Digraphs:**   Two vowels grouped together in which one sound, most often the long sound of the first vowel, is heard and the second vowel is silent; e.g., *bead, soak.* Teachers refer to this as "When two vowels go walking the first one does the talking."
- **Vowel Diphthongs:**   Sounds that are the blending of the vowel sounds; e.g., *oi* as in *spoil, oy* as in *toy, ou* as in *loud, ow* as in *crown, au* as in *August, aw* as in *flaw.*

Inventory Administration Kit

SUBSKILLS FORMAT
FORM A: PRETEST

PART 1 Graded Word Lists

Form A: Pretest   Graded Word Lists

1	this	1	came
2	her	2	day
3	about	3	big
4	to	4	house
5	are	5	after
6	you	6	how
7	he	7	put
8	all	8	other
9	like	9	went
10	could	10	just
11	my	11	play
12	said	12	many
13	was	13	trees
14	look	14	boy
15	go	15	good
16	down	16	girl
17	with	17	see
18	what	18	something
19	bank	19	little
20	on	20	saw

Form A: Pretest   Graded Word Lists

1	new		1	birthday
2	leg		2	free
3	feet		3	isn't
4	hear		4	beautiful
5	food		5	job
6	learn		6	elephant
7	hat		7	cowboy
8	ice		8	branch
9	letter		9	asleep
10	green		10	mice
11	outside		11	corn
12	happy		12	baseball
13	less		13	garden
14	drop		14	hall
15	stopping		15	pet
16	grass		16	blows
17	street		17	gray
18	page		18	law
19	ever		19	bat
20	let's		20	guess

Form A: Pretest   Graded Word Lists

1	distant		1	drain
2	phone		2	jug
3	turkeys		3	innocent
4	bound		4	relax
5	chief		5	goodness
6	foolish		6	seventeen
7	engage		7	disturb
8	glow		8	glove
9	unhappy		9	compass
10	fully		10	attractive
11	court		11	impact
12	energy		12	lettuce
13	passenger		13	operator
14	shark		14	regulation
15	vacation		15	violet
16	pencil		16	settlers
17	labor		17	polite
18	decided		18	internal
19	policy		19	drama
20	nail		20	landscape

Form A: Pretest   Graded Word Lists

1	moan		1	brisk
2	hymn		2	nostrils
3	bravely		3	dispose
4	instinct		4	headlight
5	shrill		5	psychology
6	jewel		6	farthest
7	onion		7	wreath
8	register		8	emptiness
9	embarrass		9	billows
10	graceful		10	mob
11	cube		11	biblical
12	scar		12	harpoon
13	muffled		13	pounce
14	pacing		14	rumor
15	oars		15	dazzle
16	guarantee		16	combustion
17	thermometer		17	hearth
18	zone		18	mockingbird
19	salmon		19	ridiculous
20	magical		20	widen

Form A: Pretest   Graded Word Lists

1	proven		1	utilization
2	founder		2	valve
3	motivate		3	embodiment
4	glorify		4	kidnapper
5	adoption		5	offensive
6	popper		6	ghetto
7	nimble		7	profound
8	sanitation		8	discourse
9	unstable		9	impurity
10	dispatch		10	radiant
11	pompous		11	horrid
12	knapsack		12	vastly
13	bankruptcy		13	strenuous
14	geological		14	greedy
15	stockade		15	sanctuary
16	kerchief		16	quartet
17	glisten		17	tonal
18	obtainable		18	engender
19	pyramid		19	scallop
20	basin		20	gradient

SUBSKILLS FORMAT
FORM A: PRETEST

PART 2 Graded Paragraphs

THE PLAY CAR

Tom has a play car.

His play car is red.

"See my play car," said Tom.

"It can go fast."

Ann said, "It's a big car."

"I like your car."

"Good," said Tom.

"Would you like a ride?"

OUR BUS RIDE

The children were all talking.

"No more talking, children," said Mrs. Brown.

"It is time for our trip."

"It is time to go to the farm."

Mrs. Brown said, "Get in the bus."

"Please do not push anyone."

"We are ready to go now."

The children climbed into the bus.

Away went the bus.

It was a good day for a trip.

MARIA'S PUPPIES

Maria has two puppies.

She thinks that puppies are fun to watch.

The puppies' names are *Sissy* and *Sassy*.

Puppies are born with their eyes closed.

Their ears are closed, too.

This is why they use their smell and touch.

After two weeks, puppies begin to open their eyes and ears.

Most puppies can bark after four weeks.

Maria knows that *Sissy* and *Sassy* will grow up to be good pets.

HOMEWORK FIRST

Marco and his sister Teresa love to watch TV.

The shows they like best are cartoons.

Every day after school they go outside to play.

Soon, Mother calls to them to come in.

"It's time to do your homework," she says.

"When you finish your homework you can watch your cartoons," Mother promises.

"Remember! Homework first."

Marco and Teresa are happy with this.

They do their homework.

Now they are ready to watch their cartoon shows.

THE GREAT CHICAGO FIRE

It was early October of 1871. It was very dry in Chicago. Hardly any rain had fallen between July and October. Then on the evening of October 8, 1871, a fire started in the southwest side of the city.

It is believed the fire started in a barn owned by Mrs. Patrick O'Leary. A cow kicked over a lantern in the barn. There were strong winds that night. Flames raced north and east through the city. Many families fled north to Lincoln Park. Many other families raced into the cold waters of Lake Michigan. The fire wiped out the downtown area and most north side homes killing many people.

Chicago rose from the ruins of the fire to become one of the world's greatest cities.

TIRED OF GIVING IN

It was warm that December afternoon in Montgomery, Alabama. Rosa Parks was waiting for her city bus. She was tired from a long day of work—sewing.

When her bus came, Rosa took an empty seat in the "colored" section. In 1955, blacks could not sit in the front of the bus. However, they had to give up their seats in the middle to any white left standing.

Soon the front of the bus filled up. The white driver ordered Rosa to give up her seat to a white man. She didn't move. The driver called the police. Rosa was arrested.

Almost all of Montgomery's blacks, and some whites, staged a year-long boycott of the bus system to protest Rosa's arrest. The boycott was led by Martin Luther King, Jr. It ended when the Supreme Court ruled all bus segregation illegal.

Years later, Rosa Parks said, "I didn't give up my seat because I was tired. The only tired I was, was tired of giving in."

PIRATES!

Pirates were people who attacked and robbed ships. They raided towns like Charleston, South Carolina. Most people who became pirates hoped to get rich. Most pirates were men. A few women became pirates, too.

Movies have given us the idea that pirates led exciting lives. In real life, however, most pirates led miserable lives. Many pirates died of wounds or disease. Many were captured and hanged.

In the early 1700s, pirates sailed along the coast of South Carolina. They robbed ships sailing to or from Charleston. There were so many pirates around Charleston that few ships were safe.

One of these pirates was Stede Bonnet. Bonnet was very mean. He was the first pirate to make people "walk the plank."

William Rhett set out to capture Bonnet. He did, and took Bonnet and his crew to Charleston. All of Bonnet's crew were hanged. Just before Bonnet was to be hanged, a friend took him some women's clothes. Dressed as a woman, Bonnet was able to escape. Rhett went after him again. Bonnet was brought back to Charleston and hanged.

Pirates are gone now, but their stories live on.

BORN A SLAVE

He was born a slave on a farm in Missouri. When he was still a baby, his father was killed in an accident. His mother was kidnapped by night raiders. As a child, he was raised by Moses and Susan Carver. They were his owners. They named him George Washington Carver.

Mr. and Mrs. Carver taught George as a boy to read and write. He was very eager to learn, and showed a great interest in plants. When he was eleven years old he went to a school for black children in Neosho, Missouri.

For the next 20 years, Carver worked hard to pay for his education. George became a scientist and won worldwide fame for his agricultural research. He was widely praised for his work with peanuts. He made more than 300 things from peanuts. He also spent a great deal of time helping to improve race relations.

Carver got many awards for his work. The George Washington Carver National Monument was established on 210 acres of the Missouri farm where he was born.

THE OLD ONES

There is only one place in the United States where four states meet. It is the vast Four Corners region where Arizona, Colorado, New Mexico, and Utah come together.

The Four Corners region is a beautiful landscape of canyons, of flat mesas rising above broad valleys. It is slickrock desert and red dust and towering cliffs and the lonely sky.

About 2,000 years ago, a group of men and women the Navajo people call the *Anasazi* moved into this area. *Anasazi* is a Navajo word; it means "the Old Ones."

At first, the Anasazi dug out pits, and they lived in these "pit" houses. Later, they began to build houses out of stone and adobe called *pueblos*. They built their pueblos in and on the cliffs.

The Anasazi lived in these cliff houses for centuries. They farmed corn, raised children, created pottery, and traded with other pueblos.

Now these once great pueblos have been empty since the last years of the thirteenth century, for the Anasazi walked away from homes that had been theirs for 700 years.

Who were the Anasazi? Where did they come from? Where did they go? They simply left, and the entire Four Corners region lay silent, seemingly empty for 500 years.

YOUNG, GIFTED, AND BLACK

Lorraine Hansberry was the first black American playwright to achieve critical and popular success on Broadway.

Lorraine Hansberry was born in Chicago. In 1950 she moved to New York. In 1959 she became famous for her first completed play, *A Raisin in the Sun*. With this play, she won the Drama Critics Circle award.

A Raisin in the Sun is a play, a drama, about a black family's struggle to make a better life and to escape from a Chicago ghetto. It is a study of the search for identity by black men and women, both within the family and within a racially prejudiced American society.

She followed this moving and highly successful work with another play in 1964, *The Sign in Sidney Brustein's Window.*

Lorraine Hansberry's great promise was cut short by her death from cancer in 1965. Before her death at the age of 34, she began a play about race relations in Africa.

Selections from Hansberry's letters and works were published in *To Be Young, Gifted, and Black.*

SUBSKILLS FORMAT
FORM A: POSTTEST

PART 1 Graded Word Lists

Form A: Posttest   Graded Word Lists

1	in		1	three
2	now		2	find
3	so		3	because
4	from		4	head
5	get		5	their
6	had		6	before
7	at		7	more
8	over		8	turn
9	of		9	think
10	into		10	call
11	no		11	these
12	came		12	school
13	but		13	word
14	has		14	even
15	if		15	would
16	as		16	ask
17	have		17	much
18	be		18	want
19	or		19	never
20	an		20	your

Form A: Posttest   **Graded Word Lists**

1	maybe	1	sound
2	pass	2	climb
3	out	3	waiting
4	they	4	hands
5	please	5	cry
6	love	6	doctor
7	cannot	7	people
8	eight	8	everyone
9	kind	9	strong
10	read	10	inch
11	paid	11	rock
12	open	12	sea
13	top	13	thirty
14	pool	14	dance
15	low	15	test
16	late	16	hard
17	giant	17	dogs
18	short	18	story
19	upon	19	city
20	us	20	push

Form A: Posttest   Graded Word Lists

1	computer		1	spy
2	angry		2	downtown
3	energy		3	tray
4	choice		4	lung
5	hospital		5	exhibit
6	court		6	formal
7	heard		7	weekend
8	closet		8	nineteen
9	meet		9	mixture
10	picnic		10	invitation
11	against		11	happiness
12	law		12	gulf
13	build		13	rumble
14	objects		14	plot
15	probably		15	tennis
16	shot		16	weary
17	we'll		17	lantern
18	paragraph		18	preparation
19	telephone		19	weep
20	sugar		20	jelly

Form A: Posttest　　Graded Word Lists

1	sensation		1	radiant
2	analyze		2	greatness
3	funeral		3	tardy
4	scissors		4	doughnut
5	mutual		5	armor
6	consistent		6	nurture
7	deliberately		7	dismay
8	officially		8	shipment
9	taxi		9	logic
10	parachute		10	pulley
11	radar		11	fingerprint
12	intermediate		12	jumbo
13	embarrass		13	guppy
14	raid		14	narrator
15	crude		15	crutch
16	bakery		16	shopper
17	knelt		17	punish
18	endure		18	silken
19	painful		19	omelet
20	squash		20	miniature

Form A: Posttest   Graded Word Lists

1	noisily		1	duly
2	imperative		2	furnishing
3	forge		3	emptiness
4	expressway		4	frustration
5	nominate		5	joyously
6	include		6	patriotic
7	formulate		7	zeal
8	enact		8	seriousness
9	depot		9	notorious
10	illegal		10	federation
11	distress		11	youth
12	childish		12	selection
13	unfair		13	bleak
14	sentimental		14	mutton
15	designer		15	habitation
16	luggage		16	fling
17	historically		17	dungeon
18	uncertainty		18	hierarchy
19	gardener		19	duration
20	enchant		20	journalist

SUBSKILLS FORMAT
FORM A: POSTTEST

PART 2 Graded Paragraphs

FISHING

Bob and Pam went fishing.

Bob put his line in the water.

He felt something pull on his line.

"A fish! A fish!" said Bob.

"Help me get it, Pam."

Pam said, "It's a big one."

Bob said, "We can get it."

JOSE'S FIRST AIRPLANE RIDE

Jose and his papa went to the airport.

Jose was very happy.

His papa was happy, too.

They got on the airplane.

Up high into the sky they flew.

"How high we are," said Jose.

"The cars look so small."

"And so do the houses," said Papa.

Jose said, "This is so much fun."

PLANT SPIDERS

There are all kinds of spiders.

Some spiders are big, and some spiders are small.

One kind of spider is called a plant spider.

Plant spiders are black and green in color.

Plant spiders have eight legs.

All spiders have eight legs.

Plant spiders spin their webs on plants.

That is why they are called plant spiders.

They soon learn to hunt for food and spin their webs.

THE RODEO

It is a warm, sunny day. Many people have come to the rodeo to see Bob Hill ride Midnight. Bob Hill is one of the best cowboys in the rodeo. Midnight is one of the best horses in the rodeo. He is big and fast. Midnight is a strong black horse.

The people at the rodeo stood up. They are all waiting for the big ride. Can Bob Hill ride the great horse Midnight?

GREAT WALL OF CHINA

The Chinese began work on the Great Wall about 2,000 years ago. Over time, it became the largest wall ever built. The Great Wall is about 25 feet high with watch-towers used for lookout posts. The Great Wall is almost 4,000 miles long. It was built to keep China safe from invaders from the north.

For the most part, the Great Wall kept China safe from these enemies. However, the armies of the Mongol leader Genghis Khan did cross the wall 900 years ago and conquered most of China.

Today, the Chinese no longer use the wall for defense. Visitors from all over the world come to see the Great Wall and walk the path along its top.

The Great Wall of China is the only man-made structure that can be seen by the astronauts as they orbit the earth.

THE RED KNIGHT OF GERMANY

Baron Manfred von Richthofen was known as the Red Baron or the Red Knight. *Baron* is a noble title meaning "warrior" among the early Germans. This baron was a warrior in the sky and the top ace of World War I.

An ace is an airplane pilot who shoots down at least five enemy aircraft during a war. The planes must either crash or be forced to land. During World War I, the leading aces were thought of as great heroes. They were seen as daring knights of the air.

The Red Baron shot down 80 enemy planes. He became known as the Red Knight because his plane was painted bright red. He would come flashing out of the sun. With his machine guns blazing, he forced many enemy planes to crash before their pilots knew what was happening. A plane shot down is known as a kill.

The Red Baron's streak of 80 kills came to an end when a little-known Canadian pilot, Roy Brown, shot down the Red Knight of Germany.

ZEPPELIN

It was the evening of May 6, 1937. Rain had been falling that day. The place was Lakehurst, New Jersey. More than 1,000 people had come to Lakehurst to see the airship of the future. They had come to see the great German zeppelin *Hindenburg* end a flight from Europe to the United States.

"There she is!" someone shouted. A great silver shape came out of the mist and light rain. In just a few minutes the *Hindenburg* would be ready to be tied to the mooring mast.

Two landing lines dropped down from the ship. At exactly 7:23, fire burst from the tail of the great zeppelin. The ship seemed to blow apart. In just 30 seconds, the world's greatest zeppelin lay black, broken, and smoking on Lakehurst field.

The burning of the *Hindenburg* spelled the end for the zeppelin. No more were ever built. What was supposed to be the "ship of the future" became a dead thing of the past.

ALONG THE OREGON TRAIL

Today Missouri is in the central part of the United States. In 1800, it was not the center. In those days Missouri was on the edge of the frontier. Very few people had ever seen the great lands that lay to the west of Missouri. In 1804, Captain Meriwether Lewis and William Clark set out from St. Louis to explore these lands. In November 1805, they reached the Pacific Ocean. The route they took later became known as the Oregon Trail. When they returned, Lewis and Clark told many exciting stories about the West. This made other people want to make the West their home. By the 1830s, settlers began making the long trip to the West. Missouri was the starting place for almost all these settlers. In Independence, St. Joseph, or Westport, they bought wagons, tools, and food for the two-thousand-mile trip. They went along the Oregon Trail through plains and deserts, over mountains, and across rivers.

TITANIC

The *Titanic* was the largest ship in the world. The *Titanic* was thought to be unsinkable.

On the night of April 14, 1912, the sea was calm, and the night was clear and cold. The *Titanic* was on its first trip from England to New York. The captain had received warnings of icebergs ahead. He decided to keep going at full speed and keep a sharp watch for any icebergs.

The men on watch aboard *Titanic* saw an iceberg just ahead. It was too late to avoid it. The iceberg tore a 300-foot gash in the *Titanic*'s side. The ship sank in about 2½ hours.

Of the 2,200 passengers and crew, only 705 people were saved. They were mostly women and children.

In 1985, researchers from France and the United States found the *Titanic* at the bottom of the Atlantic Ocean. Sharks and other fish now swam along the decaying decks where joyful passengers once strolled.

THE DIARY

Anne Frank, a young Jewish girl, was born in Germany in 1929. A few years after Anne's birth, Adolf Hitler and the Nazi party came to power in Germany. Germany was in a great economic depression at the time, and Hitler blamed these problems on the Jews. To escape the persecution of the Nazis, Anne and her family, like many other Jews, fled to Holland. There in Amsterdam, Anne grew up in the 1930s and early 1940s.

For her thirteenth birthday, Anne received a diary. She began writing in it. In 1942, Hitler conquered Holland, and the Nazis soon began rounding up the Jews to send them to concentration camps. Millions of Jews died in these camps.

To escape the Nazis, the Franks went into hiding. Some of their Dutch friends hid Anne and her family in some secret rooms above a warehouse in Amsterdam. In that small space the Franks lived secretly for more than two years. During that time, Anne continued to write in her diary.

By the summer of 1944, World War II was coming to an end. The American and British armies freed Holland from the Nazis, but not in time to save Anne and her family. Police discovered their hiding place and sent Anne and her family to concentration camps. Anne Frank died in the camp at Bergen-Belsen in March 1945. She was not yet sixteen years old.

All of the Franks died in the camps except Anne's father. After the war, Mr. Frank returned to Amsterdam. He revisited the small, secret rooms his family had hidden in for so long. Among the trash and broken furniture, he found Anne's diary.

READER RESPONSE FORMAT
FORM B: PRETEST

Graded Paragraphs

IT'S MY BALL

Tom and Nancy went for a walk.

They saw a small ball on the grass.

They began fighting over the ball.

While they were fighting, a dog picked up the ball and ran.

The kids ran after the dog, but the dog got away.

FISH FOR SALE

Susan got ten fish and a tank for her birthday.

She loved the fish and learned to take good care of them.

One day, Susan saw six new baby fish in the tank.

The fish tank was too small for all of the fish.

Dad said he would buy another tank for the baby fish.

Everyone began giving Susan fish and equipment.

Soon she had tanks for big fish, small fish, and baby fish.

Each tank had water plants, air tubes, and stones on the bottom.

Mom said, "Enough! Susan, your room looks like a store for fish."

That gave Susan an idea. Why not put all of the fish tanks in the garage and put up a sign?

Susan and her dad moved everything into the garage.

Susan made a big sign that read, "FISH FOR SALE."

SILLY BIRDS

With food all around them, baby turkeys will not eat. They don't know food when they see it. They often die for lack of water. Water is always kept in their bowls, but some of these birds never seem to discover what the water is for. We have a hard time trying to understand these silly birds.

Baby turkeys don't know enough to come out of the rain either. So many of the silly young birds catch cold and die. If they see anything bright, they will try to eat it. It may be a coin, a small nail, or even a shovel. You can see how foolish these silly birds are.

ALONG THE OREGON TRAIL

This is a story about one family that traveled along the Oregon Trail. We will call this family the Mortons. Their son, Andrew, wrote this journal with the help of his sister, Emily. Here are some entries from Andrew's journal.

March 31, 1848:	Hurray! Today we leave St. Louis and take a steamboat up the Missouri River to Independence, Missouri. Emily can hardly stop talking.
April 7, 1848:	Today we arrived in Independence. Emily asked Pa how long the trip would take from here. He told her six months.
May 5, 1848:	The wagonmaster told us to keep a sharp lookout for Indians. Emily says she's not afraid.
June 16, 1848:	Tomorrow we reach Fort Laramie. Ma said we've come more than 700 miles.
July 11, 1848:	We are now climbing up the Rocky Mountains. The nights are cold.
July 20, 1848:	We have come down from the mountains. The weather is scorching hot.
August 15, 1848:	Today we reached Fort Hall. The soldiers gave us antelope steaks and turnips for dinner. Emily says she hates turnips.
November 12, 1848:	We are near the Willamette River Valley. We shall soon see the place where we will make our new home. Emily calls this the promised land.

THE FOX—A FARMER'S BEST FRIEND

"Meg, look! That's a female fox ready to have cubs." Uncle Mike was excited, "I haven't seen a fox around here for ten years." Meg said, "Shall I get your gun?" "There's no need for a gun," Uncle Mike replied. "Foxes help farmers by eating pests like mice, squirrels, frogs, and insects."

The next day Meg and her uncle were unhappy to learn that some farmers were hunting for the fox. These farmers didn't believe that a fox was helpful. Foxes save the farmers' crops by eating pests that destroy their crops. The farmers were sure that foxes only killed chickens and other small animals.

After weeks of hunting, the farmers gave up trying to kill the fox. When Uncle Mike and Meg found fresh fox and cub tracks on the far end of their farm, they were pleased the fox had not been killed.

HUSH MY BABY

Nate was a slave who lived with his master in Baltimore. Nate wanted freedom. He got an idea. "What if I build a big box, big enough so I could hide in it?" Nate got busy, and when the box was built, he got inside of it. Nate's uncle put the box on a ship that was going to New York. It was very cold in the box. Nate was afraid he would not make it to freedom.

On a Sunday morning, the ship arrived in New York. Nate's friend John was waiting at the dock. The ship's captain told John they didn't deliver boxes on Sunday. John worried that Nate might die from being in the box too long. He talked the captain into letting him take the box with him.

While the captain was helping John load the box onto a wagon, Nate sneezed. John was afraid that Nate would be discovered and sent back to his owner. To cover the noise of Nate's sneeze, John started singing "Hush My Baby." This also warned Nate to be very quiet. At last the box was delivered to the right house.

It was opened, and out popped Nate, cold and stiff—but happy and free!

THE GOLDEN DOOR

The year was 1892. A ship crowded with people from many parts of the world was nearing New York City.

Jacob Goldberg stood at the ship's rail waiting. Jacob and his family were forced to leave their home in Russia because of the violent anti-Jewish attacks that took place there.

Beside Jacob at the ship's rail stood Nunzio Genetti. Nunzio and Jacob had become friends during the long sea voyage, even though neither one could speak the other's language. Nunzio and his family had to leave their small village in Italy because there was no work for the people.

As the ship came into New York Harbor, the boys' eyes widened. There, in the middle of the harbor, stood the *Lady with the Lamp*—the Statue of Liberty.

Many people crowded the rail beside Jacob and Nunzio. They began crying and cheering at the same time.

Surely, here was the *Golden Door* through which to pass to a better life.

THE WORLD OF DINOSAURS

Before the 1800s, no one knew that dinosaurs had ever existed. Once in a while, people would find a dinosaur tooth or bone, but did not realize what it was.

When dinosaurs lived, the earth was not like it is today. Mountains like the Alps, for example, had not yet been formed.

The first dinosaur appeared on the earth about 220 million years ago. For 150 million years or so, they ruled the earth. Suddenly, about 63 million years ago, dinosaurs died out.

What caused this "terrible lizard," for that is what *dinosaur* means in English, to die out so suddenly?

Scientists have developed lots of theories to try to explain what happened to the dinosaurs. One theory is that the earth became too cold for them.

Most scientists believe that no single theory explains what happened to the dinosaurs. It may be that they could not keep up with the way the earth was changing. Whatever the cause, or causes, it was the end of the World of Dinosaurs.

READER RESPONSE FORMAT
FORM B: POSTTEST

Graded Paragraphs

THE RED ANT

The red ant lives under the sand.

The ant must build its own room.

It has to take the sand outside.

The sand is made into little hills.

Building a room is hard work.

The red ant is a busy bug.

WHY CAN'T I PLAY?

Kim wanted to play on the boys' team.

The boys said, "No."

One day, the boys needed one more player.

They asked Kim to play.

Kim got the ball and kicked it a long way.

She was a fast runner and a good player.

Todd, a boy on the team, kicked the ball to her.

Kim kicked the ball down the side of the field.

Tony, a boy on the other team, tried to block her.

He missed, and Kim scored.

Someone said, "Kim should have played on the team all year."

FLOODS ARE DANGEROUS

Mrs. Sanchez was driving home with her two sons, Luis and Ernesto. From the darkening sky, Mrs. Sanchez could see that a storm was coming. Soon, lightning flashed, thunder boomed, and the rain poured down. In order to get to her house, Mrs. Sanchez had to cross a road covered with water. She decided to drive across the rushing water. When they were just about across the road, the rising water caused the car to float away. Mrs. Sanchez knew that she had to get the boys and herself out of that car.

Luis was able to roll down the window and jump to dry ground. Mrs. Sanchez also jumped to some dry ground. Mrs. Sanchez and Luis tried to grab Ernesto, but the car floated out of reach.

Soon the police and some friends came, and they searched all night for Ernesto and the car. They were unable to find them. Had Ernesto drowned in the flood, or was he safe?

Early the next day, Mrs. Sanchez saw a police car drive up to her house. Her heart raced when she saw Ernesto in the police car. He was safe! Ernesto told his mother that their car got stuck against a tree and that he was able to climb out of the car. He sat in the tree until daylight when the police saw him. Everyone was happy to see Ernesto again.

FIRST TO DIE

It was very cold that March day in Boston. The year was 1770. It was a time of protest and riots. The people of Boston had had it with British rule.

Nobody knew that the day would end in bloodshed. This was the day of the Boston Massacre—March 5, 1770.

Somewhere in the city that night, a black man and former slave named Crispus Attucks was moving toward his place in history.

The British had brought troops into Boston in 1768. There were fights between the people of Boston and the soldiers.

On the night of March 6, 1770, the streets were filled with men. They were angry. Crispus Attucks was the leader of a patriot crowd of men. They met up with a group of British soldiers. The crowd pushed in on the soldiers. There was much confusion. A soldier fired his rifle. Attucks fell into the gutter—dead.

Crispus Attucks had been a leader in the night's actions. A black man and a former slave, he had helped to bring about action that led to the foundation of American independence.

TIGER

Tiger is hungry. He has not eaten for five days. His last meal was a wild pig. It is dark now, and Tiger is on a hunt. As he slinks through the jungle, the muscles of his powerful neck and shoulders are tense. Tiger senses that there are humans close by. Tiger is careful to avoid humans. He knows that only old or sick tigers will hunt humans because they are no longer swift enough to hunt other animals.

Suddenly, Tiger's sensitive nostrils pick up the scent of an animal. Tiger creeps slowly toward the smell. There, in a clearing in the jungle, he sees a goat. The goat has picked up Tiger's scent. Tiger moves in, but the goat does not flee. It is a trap! Humans have tied the goat there to trap Tiger. Tiger stops, then moves back into the jungle.

Tiger is hungry.

SENTINELS IN THE FOREST

Many wild creatures that travel with their own kind know by instinct how to protect the group. One of them acts as a sentinel.

Hidden by the branches of a low-hanging tree, I once watched two white-tailed deer feeding in a meadow. At first, my interest was held by their beauty. But soon I noticed something strange; they were taking turns feeding. While one was calmly cropping grass, unafraid and at ease, the other—with head high, eyes sweeping the sea marsh, and sensitive nostrils "feeling" the air—stood on guard against enemies. Not for a moment, during the half hour I spied upon them, did they stop their teamwork.

I LOVE A MYSTERY

Ever since the year 1841, when Edgar Allan Poe wrote *The Murders in the Rue Morgue,* people around the world quickly become fans of the mystery/detective story.

The mystery begins with a strange crime. There are a number of clues. A detective is called in to solve the mysterious crime. The clues may lead the detective to or away from the solution. In the end the detective reveals the criminal and tells how the mystery was solved.

The detective in most mystery stories is usually not a regular police officer but a private detective. Probably the most famous of all these private detectives is Sherlock Holmes. With his friend and assistant Dr. Watson, Sherlock Holmes solved many strange crimes.

One of the most popular of all the mysteries that Holmes solved is called *The Hound of the Baskervilles.* In this story a man is murdered, and the only clue Holmes has to go on is an enormous hound's footprints found next to the dead man's body.

Do you love a mystery?

IT CANNOT BE HELPED

There is a phrase the Japanese use when something difficult must be endured—*it cannot be helped.*

On a quiet Sunday morning in early December 1941, the Japanese launched a surprise attack on Pearl Harbor. Shortly after that, the Army and the FBI began rounding up all Japanese who were living along the West Coast of the United States. Every Japanese man, woman, and child, 110,000 of them, was sent to inland prison camps. Even though the Japanese had been living in the United States since 1869, they were never allowed to become citizens. Suddenly, they were a people with no rights who looked exactly like the enemy.

With the closing of the prison camps in the fall of 1945, the families were sent back to the West Coast.

The Japanese relocation program, carried through at such great cost in misery and tragedy, was justified on the ground that the Japanese were potentially disloyal. The record does not show a single case of Japanese disloyalty or sabotage during the whole war.

In June 1952, Congress passed Public Law 414, granting Japanese the right to become United States citizens.